Sol

Sol Searching

A Fun-filled Tale of a Modern
Girl's Move To The Costa del Sol

Keidi Keating

NativeSpain.™com

First Published in 2008 through Lulu as 'Sol Searching'

This Edition Published 2009 by
Native Spain (www.nativespain.com)

Typeset in Book Antiqua

**Although this book is based on real events and
characters, some names, descriptions and details
have been changed to protect identities.**

Dedicated to David Foulkes, who passed away on 3rd September, 2009, aged 70. Dave encouraged me to get The Sentinella magazine off the ground, allowing me unlimited usage of his office and its facilities. His entrepreunial qualities and enviable energy, gave me the kick-start I needed to launch and later grow The Sentinella to the success it is today. So thank you Dave. Peace be with you.

Praise For Sol Searching

An enlightening and humorous journey of a determined young lady, with the guts to turn her dream into a reality. I laughed so hard at certain chapters I nearly fell off my chair. I only hope there'll be a part two.

Steve Hall, www.thisisspain.info

Sol Searching is the unusual tale of a young woman battling the odds to create a new life for herself in Spain, whilst setting up a successful new magazine. Brutally honest and engaging, Sol Searching should be read by anyone thinking of moving to a different country.

Nick Snelling, author of Taking The Heat and How To Sell Your Spanish Property in a Crisis, www.nicholassnelling.com

This is an honest account of one girl's arrival in Spain. It's observational, self-deprecating, has some great characters and many laugh out loud moments. It's written in a similar style to the Sentinella, because after all we all have a certain writing voice, and Keidi honours that. Most people like the Sentinella because it's fun and light-hearted and this is exactly what Sol Searching is. I admire anyone who sits down a writes and book and then goes on to publish it, so well done Keidi.

Hannah Davis

Sol Searching is a great way to switch off and de-stress. I would recommend it to everyone. Keidi Keating is an A* writer, thanks for sharing your move to Spain with us.

Peter Williams

Well done Keidi, your book is great. I couldn't stop giggling from the time I picked it up till the end of Chapter 24. I love your light-hearted approach and some of your character descriptions. I hope you'll be writing more books in the future.

Mandy Rogers

This is an excellent, read - one I could not put down until I had finished the last page only yesterday. It had me laughing, crying and nodding in agreement throughout. I can relate well to this book, being a similar age to Keidi and having moved to Singapore on my own to start a new life adventure. Many of the quirky stories I can relate to so well, as I am sure many other 20 somethings can, whether living in a new country or not! This book has inspired me to continue living out my dreams abroad. Well done Keidi on a book well written. I look forward to reading more in the future.

Mary Clauster

Acknowledgements

To my fab parents, Patrick and Roisheen, who are always there for me when I need them most. *The Sentinella* would not have happened without their constant help, advice and guidance. Also, if they had not moved to Spain in the first place, neither would I! So "thank you" a million times to the best parents in the world.

To my boyfriend Chema, who I love with all my heart. He waltzed into my life at the right time, and is the most amazing man I have ever known. Thank you *mi novio perfecto* for making me feel so alive and very happy.

To my sister and brother-in-law, Kami and Tony Knight, who have done an amazing job in taking over the day to day running of *The Sentinella* magazine. I could not have offered the position to a more efficient and professional hubbie and wife team.

To my nieces Charli and Leoni Knight, who always bring a smile to my face. Lots of love to you! X

To my 'writer friend' Hannah Davis (aka Anna), who helped me edit *Sol Searching* to a sensible size. We have shared many fun-filled adventures. I wish Hannah the greatest luck with her novel.

To my friends Liz Armer, Nicole Squires, Emma Travers-Spencer and Leigharnagh Garrard, who I enjoy lengthy phone conversations with about my life in Spain. Thanks to you all for helping me to stay sane during the tough times.

To all the advertisers in *The Sentinella* magazine, past, present and future. It is your support which has enabled the magazine to succeed. Equal thanks to *The Sentinella* readers. Carry on laughing at all those jokes!

Foreword

Escaping the hamster wheel of daily life in your home country is the stuff of dreams for millions. Keidi Keating is one of those who turned the dream into reality. Choosing to cut all ties with her life in London, Keidi moved lock, stock and barrel to southern Spain. Five years later and she's still there.

As Keidi quickly discovers, life in Spain isn't all a bed of rosas. Even on the sun-drenched Costa del Sol, it can pour with rain, jobs are few and far between and well-paid ones almost non-existent. The expat community is a weird mix and making lasting friendships can be as frustrating as finding a good job. But if you stick it out and Keidi does, Spain is a land of opportunities. After five years on her Spanish roller coaster, Keidi has found plenty.

Moving abroad is probably one of the most challenging things life can throw at you, but with perseverance, the right attitude and a bit of luck, it's also one of life's most rewarding as Keidi finds out. This refreshing and light-hearted look at relocation is a welcome addition to the many books on Spain. Enjoy!

Joanna Styles

Joanna Styles also successfully relocated to southern Spain where she has lived for the last 20 years. Joanna is a freelance writer and the author of several books on relocation and Spain. Contact her at *www.joannastyles.com*

Contents

Introduction

Dear Lord/Buddha/Higher Being,

Thank you for giving me the opportunity to move to Spain.

Please help me to find a job, so I can earn a living here.

Please also help me make some friends so I don't continue getting on my parents nerves.

I wouldn't mind meeting a man too – a good looking hunk if possible!

Thank you Lord/Buddha/Higher Being,

Amen

When I landed in Málaga on March the twenty-sixth 2004 I had no job, no friends, no man and no car. All I had were my trusty parents and a roof over my head. Five years later I have my own apartment, a new car, an amazing man, family, friends, a thriving business, and lots of plans for the future. My life has changed enormously. It took a mound of stamina, effort and tears, but I finally feel that I have reached the point I once only dreamt about. Now I can look back and reflect.

Before the upheaval I could not face the bad weather and daily rituals in the UK any more I had to break free. I planned to move to Spain, but was I being too hasty?

Had I thought this life-changing move through properly? Would I grow to miss the things I hated? Would I grow to hate the ways of life I thought I would love? Was I, in fact, seeking escape from my own problems and issues, rather than from the UK itself? Was it all too easy to say "I hate the weather, I hate the politics, I hate the people," rather than "I hate *my* life?"

My answers to all of those questions can be found in the coming chapters, but one thing is for certain; my moving-abroad experience took me on a journey, a fulfilling path of self-discovery. Along the way I had my fair share of both soul strengthening and soul destroying experiences and endured a bumpy journey on my mission to meet Mr Right. *Sol Searching* is written from a very personal point of view, to give others an idea of what to expect when moving abroad. It is important to remember though, that everyone's voyage will be different.

I am one of a growing trend of youngsters who choose to dwell in sunnier climes. In earlier times those who moved abroad were more often than not retirees, seeking a better life-style during their latter days. They had worked hard all their lives and sought rest and a sprinkling of the good life; the sun, the sea, the serenity and the chance to de-stress and unwind from the hardships of life in England. These retirees had typically paid off their mortgages, sold their properties and relocated to Spain with enough money in the bank to buy a nice pad with sufficient cash left over to live on. Most had pensions too and the chance to live in a country with lower living costs; the opportunity for their pension money to stretch further each month.

Now it is not just the older generation who seek a less stressful life. There are an increasing number of twenty and thirty-somethings, singles, couples and some with young families, who dream of greener pastures.

In the year 2005, two-hundred thousand Brits moved overseas, equal to one every three minutes. It is estimated that a further one million will move over the next five years. Australia is the most popular destination, but Spain falls a close second, with more than seven-hundred and sixty thousand now resident.

When youngsters move to Spain they need something that retirees don't – a job! I was dealt a lucky hand and landed a life-changing opportunity by pure fate. For others, it isn't so simple, and finding suitable employment is tough. Unemployment results in uncertainty, stress, a lack of money, and for some the need to return to the UK; back to where it all started. The dreams crushed by reality.

What makes us 'young ones' jump on a plane and wave goodbye to our homeland in the first place? Well, there are a whole host of reasons. A number want to escape from dark nights and cold days. Others feel the UK can not offer them the life they desire. A few have family and friends already living in Spain and would like to join them. For some, moving abroad is not a means of escape, but a route of discovery to seek new adventures and experiences. Many simply can't afford to take their first step on to the housing ladder in the UK, where prices have spiralled in recent years, whereas property in Spain is still relatively affordable. Then there are those, like me, who's decisions encompass all the above.

Perhaps it is the disintegration of values and quality of life in the UK, such as yob culture and binge drinking, which are compelling more youngsters to head for Spain.

If you are patriotic, you may find the introduction to this book somewhat offensive, but please remember those were my thoughts at the time. You may find it interesting how I interpret the same thoughts later in the book.

Before you launch into my account, I'll briefly introduce you to my family and the area in which I lived in the UK. My parents' house, where I spent nineteen years of my life, was an average four-bed semi, in the suburban outskirts of Bromley in Kent.

Roisheen, my Mum, is the homely type; a beautiful and intelligent lady in her late fifties, who doesn't look a day over forty. She is slender, pale skinned and softly spoken, with long dark hair. In the UK she worked as a childminder and now she enjoys looking after her two grandchildren.

Patrick, my Father, is a great people-person who oozes energy. He loves playing tennis and watching sport, especially football. He is a healthy, slim man with a huge appetite. In the UK he ran a tailors shop with his brother in London. Now he hosts a quiz at a local English bar and likes nothing more than relaxing with a coffee. Other relatives and characters will be introduced throughout *Sol Searching*. All have inspired and helped me in various ways, as I hope this book inspires and helps you.

Adios Old, Hola New

I had left it all behind. Everything I had grown to hate, but there were also the parts I loved, and I had left those behind too. I had waved goodbye to it all to live a deep-rooted dream.

Life in England was never my cup of char. I hated having to pay sky-high council tax bills, while swerving around potholes in the road. I loathed inhaling BO-soaked armpits on the London Underground. I cringed at office politics, which involved leaving work thirty minutes after "going-home time" just to score brownie points with the boss. I even hated drinking like a fish on Saturday nights, just because there was nothing better to do. I detested seeing Anne Robinson's wink every time I switched on the box. I despised grease-drenched fish & chips, and I couldn't stand the way Mr Blair's mug plagued the daily rags. One thing was for sure. I was certainly not a patriotic kind of girl.

Some may say I had an easy life, as I scraped my way on to the housing ladder at the tender age of 19, even if that did mean living in Dratford (oops, Dartford)!

"Isn't that where there's a tunnel?" was a frequent speculation.

Apart from the famous tunnel, all Dartford offered was a Co-op and an assortment of 'Everything for a Pound' stores.

I even had a boyfriend, who had an unhealthy liking for satirical American TV programmes I can't stand.

Despite this, he loved my wayward brown hair with a mind of its own; my dark eyes, which watered too much around onions; and my thin body, which I thought looked scrawny. He even loved my determined nature, my erratic moods and my dangerously high energy levels.

I was a writer for a corporate communications company in the West End of London. Sounds glamorous, but in reality it meant writing constant bullshit to make companies appear better than they really were. The words 'strategy', 'initiative' and 'incentive' had to feature in every story. Most of the staff of these companies (including management) would fold their free newsletters into aeroplanes before propelling them into the nearest bin.

I felt that life had gone stale. I felt that I had gone stale. I needed a change and I needed one pronto! Fortunately, the events that followed led to a fateful path of opportunity, adventure and insight.

"We're flying to Spain to look for a property," said my Dad out the blue. He had taken early retirement and was looking for an investment opportunity.

"You may as well move out there," I said, without looking up from my book. "At your ages you should be enjoying life, not stuck living in the same house for another four decades."

My Mum had no intentions of moving to Spain, as she was as anti-sun as you can get. She was insistent that exposing her wrinkle-free skin to such climates would cause an outbreak of old age.

"I haven't spent all these years taking care of myself to end up looking like a wrinkly old prune," she said, grinning, but when they returned to their four-bed semi, there was a fresh spring to their step.

They purchased an apartment on the tenth floor of a block, overlooking the coastal resort of Torre del Mar on the Costa del Sol, in an area known as Axarquia.

"Guess what? We're moving to Spain after all," said my Dad with a broad smile. "We'll be leaving in a few months."

A wave of light enveloped my body. The thought 'I also want to move to Spain' darted into my head and it made no attempt to leave. So, using my cunning intuition, I decided to sell my lovely flat to purchase an even lovelier apartment in a far lovelier part of the world. I bagged a buyer within just two weeks. My flat-mate moved into a two-bed house, so we reversed the roles and it was my turn to rent a room from her.

I wasted no time booking a short trip to Spain, with the intention of buying a property, and immediately adored the busy atmosphere that Torre del Mar exuded. I could see why my folks had decided to move into their apartment with it's amazing sea views; a blanket of deep blue, adorned with a zillion boats, and edged by a tranquil beach with gently swaying palm trees. It sure beat views of a burnt out Skoda surrounded by a clan of hoodies sniffing illegal substances!

Torre del Mar is relatively large in comparison to many towns on the eastern Costa del Sol. Fifteen years ago it was a tiny fishing port, but it now buzzes throughout the week and has become a working town, enjoying constant improvements. There is a handy tram link, and further housing areas are appearing left, right and centre. The beach is vast and never too crowded and the promenade is the longest on the Costa del Sol.

There were just ten days to find a place to buy. I viewed lots of grot-spots and a couple of possibilities, but it wasn't until the penultimate day that, rather like men, two turned up at once. Firstly a five-bedroom town house in Algarrobo Pueblo, a small village five minutes inland from the coast. The exterior walls were pink (my favourite colour) and all rooms were spacious and refurbished. It was a serious contender. The second option was a one-bedroom apartment in El Morche, a small coastal area sandwiched between the larger towns of Torre del Mar and Nerja. The apartment was new-build, so I was shown around a half-finished shell. I agonised over a list of the pros and cons of each property, until finally I reached a sensible decision.

"I'm going to put in an offer for the new build," I told my parents. "After all, the beach is closer…"

The apartment would take another three months or so to build and even when it was finished I didn't plan to move in straight-away. It was just nice to know it was there, ready for me when I chose to buy a one way ticket to Spain.

The initial stages of the buying process were easy as the estate agent and solicitor deal with the paperwork between them. In my case, buying a new-build property wasn't too complex and I didn't need a huge mortgage as I had made a profit on my flat in Dartford. Signing the contract in Spain happens a lot faster than in the UK, where 'chains' are the norm.

Back in England, I couldn't stop smiling. I broke the news to my friends straight away.

"I can't believe you've actually done it," said my best friend. I couldn't either.

My boyfriend was far from impressed and our relationship began to deteriorate. We split up a few weeks later.

The next chain of events made me feel as if a force from above was giving me a very strong shove in a particular direction. Firstly, the job. One overcast day as I counted the cracks in the wall for the fifth time that hour my boss called me to his office.

"I'm sorry Keidi" he said, shaking his head without looking me in the eye. "The business is in turmoil and we no longer have a place for you here. Clear your desk tonight please."

I wanted to move to Spain on the spot, but the timing was all wrong. After all, my apartment wasn't ready and I hadn't sorted out work there. I had no other option than to search for another job in the UK. Two days later I landed a freelance position and the daily rate was brilliant. However, my colleagues were a mundane and lifeless bunch, and I felt like shooting myself when I realised I had to endure another four days, seven hours, twelve minutes and forty-five seconds before the week was up. When it was, my boss offered me a full-time contract. I felt sick. The thought of working indefinitely there was unbearable, but a rising mortgage meant I had no choice than to sit full-time amongst the John Majors of Corporate Communications. Somehow I managed to plough through the days ahead until I couldn't stand it any more. All I could think about was Spain. Six weeks later I handed in my notice and planned to move there, job or no job. The colleagues didn't seem at all ruffled to hear I was leaving, apart from the girl who handed me the press releases.

"I'm really going to miss you," she said in an exaggerated voice.

'I bet you will,' I thought.

Then something marvellous happened. I received a phone call from a businessman in Spain, who wanted to interview me for the position of Editor. It took a few milliseconds to remember that I had applied for a job near Marbella, a couple of months ago.

9

"Sorry it has taken me so long to get in touch," he said. "I'm in London at the moment, so are you free on Wednesday for an interview?"

'This is it' I thought as I perched on a Starbucks chair. 'This is *the* job which is going to bring me to a new and fantastic life in Spain'.

The man was not at all what I expected. He was young, handsome, and he made no attempt to hide that he had dosh and lots of it. His magazine was one of those glossy sorts, packed with adverts from prestigious designer companies, such as Armani and Gucci. The average reader most likely owned a stunning penthouse in the heart of Marbella, at least two fast sports cars, and probably a yacht. I switched on my floozy girlie act and he took to me straight away (always works!).

"When will you let me know your decision?" I asked, twirling a strand of hair around my finger with my most seductive face.

"Well I have another few people to see," he said. "But out of everyone I've seen already let's just say the rest are all idiots."

He winked at me somewhat perversely then jumped in a black cab, leaving me to walk to the station in the rain.

Soon my parents were ready to say "adiós". There we all were. The entire family sat together in the living room for the last time. We had done it all in there. Coloured pictures, had fights, jumped on Dad, thrown tantrums, watched films, played catch with Mum's ornaments. Everything! It was a moment I will never forget, as my entire childhood flew in front of my eyes and I realised how precious time is. When my teary-eyed parents said their final goodbye, I knew it wouldn't be long before I saw them again.

A week later, I rang Mr Money to find out whether he had made a decision about the job.

"Oh did I forget to ring you," he said, as cool as a cucumber. "The job's yours, but I'm not sure about a starting date yet. I'll let you know about that."

When he hung up I jumped up and down screaming with joy. I was so excited and I didn't give a flying monkey that the whole of Oxford Street thought I was a mad-woman. Even the rain-sodden *Big Issue* seller stole a sly smirk.

I rang my parents that night.

"I'm coming to live out there and I need somewhere to stay until my apartment is ready. It'll probably only be for a week or so, then I can move into my own place."

They were overjoyed that their youngest offspring was joining them in Spain. I was over the moon that I had somewhere to stay. But at that moment none of us realised that 'one week' would turn into a much longer period of time. In fact one week turned into nine months (an entire pregnancy) and it wasn't going to be an easy nine months at that. I had just two weeks to arrange a transfer of my entire life.

It was a stressful time, but everything came together in the end. My sister agreed to store some things in her loft that I couldn't bear to throw out, my uncle let me leave my Ford Ka on his drive and my flatmate promised to keep my favourite plant alive.

When the plane touched down, the first thing I saw out of the window was the sun shining brightly. "Only the end of March, yet already nice and warm" I thought. "This is definitely the right move. Finally my new life has begun."

First Days

After unpacking as many of my clothes as possible on to the square metre of neighbouring bed available, I prayed I wouldn't have to stay in this clutter for too long.

"Sorry your room is such a mess," said my Mum, sighing. "We still have loads of boxes to unpack and there's nowhere else to put them."

"No worries," I said, almost tripping over a spare mattress.

Living with my parents again felt like I had taken a step back in life, but I knew it was a necessary hindrance. In the depths of my mind I knew this regression was only a temporary measure, but it was still difficult and I envisaged an onslaught of arguments. Initially my row-ometer was hovering on a fairly safe two out of ten, but the slightest hiccup could start it rising.

"Fetch me your washing, I'm putting on a load" yelled my Mum at 9.04am.

"And do you want toast or porridge for breakfast? Orange or apple juice?" My reaction was not dissimilar to that of a pre-pubescent teenager.

"What?" I shouted back, still picking sleep from my eyes. Dirty washing and a breakfast menu were the last things on my mind. It was my first morning in Spain for Pete's sake! Deep down I knew my sweet Mum was only trying her hardest to be accommodating, so I should have been thankful.

In addition to the 'lack of independence' issue, there was a far worse problem occurring. That large round fiery ball, called the sun, was playing a rather typically timed game of Hide 'n Seek. It is a well-known fact that its always sunny in Spain (for three hundred and twenty days a year according to the holiday brochures), but it was just my rotten luck that Miss Sun had decided to quit the shining, replaced by moody grey clouds chucking down cats and dogs. The kind of 'I'm not gonna budge for days clouds' which if featured in an illustrated book would wear solemn, frowning faces to mirror their macho arrogance. I wondered what had become of the saying, "the rain in Spain falls mainly on the plain". I hadn't even packed my brolly. I didn't think I would need it.

In England I lost around six a year, all left (still dripping) down the side of a train seat, forgotten after a brain cell depleting journey with bundles of damp, soulless commuters. The following day I would pay a trip to Lost Property at London Bridge.

"Can you describe your umbrella?" a scary Gothic-style teenager would ask from behind a crumb littered desk.

"Umm, black." I would state, wondering how else to describe an umbrella apart from the colour.

"Take your pick," she would respond pulling out a tray of twenty-three.

"That's the one, thanks," I would answer, grabbing a cool button operated version, far better than my wind damaged job.

Now I didn't have the fun of stealing other people's umbrellas. My game didn't exist and that saddened me somewhat. Instead, I watched the raindrops trickle down the balcony doors.

"I may as well move back to the UK if this rain continues" I told my Mum, who was ironing a pile of Dad's T-shirts.

"It's only March," she reminded me. "Spain has a winter too remember. It isn't hot and sunny all year round." I snorted like a pot-bellied pig and drank my orange juice.

Later that morning, as there was nothing better to do than build an ark and find two of every animal to take aboard, I joined my parents on their weekly outing to a local charity group.

"Spot the person under the age of fifty" I thought scanning the room. The group was holding a sale of disintegrating tat to raise funds for the centre. I glanced at the sorry looking possessions on show.

"How about this vase for your new apartment?" asked my Mum, trying to transform a bad situation into a good.

The vase in question looked like it belonged in a museum or other place of historical significance. It was even turning that rotten yellow colour, which is a frequent vision on *The Antiques Roadshow*. I rolled my eyes and shuffled to the fairy cake stall to lift my dampened spirits by eating. It was very disappointing, when after months anticipating a new and fab life in Spain I resorted to being chatted up by wrinkly retirees. Walking sticks, varicose veins, false teeth and purple rinse weren't on my 'hot topic' conversation list.

"You can always join our knitting club if you're looking for something to do," said an old dear, who introduced herself as Deirdre. "I'm making a beautiful crocheted cardigan at the moment in blue. I already have one in grey…"

"I have six great grandchildren you know?" croaked a ninety-six year old called Vera, rummaging through her brown leather handbag. "Let's see if I can find some photos. They're so adorable. Katie, the eldest, is doing ever so well at school. They think she's a genius, would you believe?"

I feigned a smile, but I wasn't in the least interested.

"Would you like a mint?" she continued, leaning on her walking stick.

"No. Thank you," I said glaring at the rotting packet, which appeared to have been purchased in 1982.

Where were all the young people to talk about Big Brother, that new flavour of vodka and who shagged who in last night's episode of Sex and the City?

As the morning progressed I became tired of grey hair and wrinkles. I had put on a false 'I'm happy' front all morning, so when we said "adiós" to a hundred and one oldies, I was relieved to revert to a moaning daughter.

"That was boring," I told my parents. "I'm never going there again, ever. Not even if I'm still around when I'm eighty. I'd rather sit and watch paint dry…slowly."

My Dad chuckled. My Mum remained silent. I think she was mentally debating whether Nancy's leg was as false as it looked.

Were there any young English people in Spain apart from me?

The writer in me was bursting to share my treacherous first morning in Spain with my pals in England, but my parents had not yet invested in the Internet, so e-mailing friends meant using the local bank where there was a free computer set up especially for clients. We bumped into a man there, who also fitted into the 'old' category, which was emerging as a trend.

"This is Len," introduced my Dad. "Len runs a bar here in Torre del Mar. And Len, this is Keidi, my daughter. She has just moved here and she's looking for a job."

"I'd love to offer you a position in my bar," said Len with a smile. "But I don't have anything suitable at the moment. The restaurant just up the road is looking for a part time waitress. You ought to check that out. Tell them I sent you." Due to his overwhelming height, I nicknamed Len 'Lofty Len'.

At the bank I wrote to my friends, revealing how utterly miserable I was. I also e-mailed Mr Money, who had offered me a job at his magazine, near Marbella. He said he would call with a starting date, but I thought I'd remind him. While awaiting his response I decided to try and land any old job just to keep the cash flow positive.

The restaurant Lofty Len mentioned had the really imaginative name of *Sue and Pete's*. It didn't look like it had seen a mop in days and inside everything was tacky. Union Jack flags littered the walls, along with football memorabilia and other random items that meant nothing to anyone but Sue and Pete. It reminded me of one of those seaside cafes on Brighton seafront. In Brighton it's all very well, but in the middle of Torre del Mar, the place was an eyesore. Unfortunately, or perhaps fortunately in hindsight, Sue put me off the job. The thought of her as my boss was about as appealing as working for Bin Laden as a beard groomer. She was the stereotypical 'Fag-Ash scrubber'. Ms Fag-Ash planted her oversized butt on to the stool next to me. In between blowing clouds of smoke into my face, bursting into coughing fits and showering me with flecks of spit, she spoke.

"You have to tie your hair back. You have to wear white. You have to pull your weight. And if the toilets need cleaning, someone's got to do them you know…."

It suddenly dawned on me that I have trouble putting a cup of tea down without spilling it, so the thought of carrying four fry-ups to the table put me off. Who knows where the fried eggs would end up? Probably over Fag-Ash Sue's head if she continued speaking to me like that. And as for the bog-brush, well, I would be more than tempted to drag it through her matted hair.

"Thanks for your kind offer of work," I said, a tad sarcastically. "But the job's not really for me. Good luck finding someone else."

"How did it go?" asked my Mum back at home.

"Terrible," I said, dropping on to the sofa, feeling utterly destroyed.

"I'm a writer. I can't clean bogs and serve dinners for a living."

"You knew all that before you moved here," said my mother, extracting a lasagne from the oven.

"I know, but I need to make some friends too. At the moment I don't have anything."

"Your trouble is you want everything too soon," said my Mum, dumping lasagne on to plates. "You've only been here a day. Things don't happen over-night. If you're going to think like that, you may as well go home now."

She had a point.

The next day the weather took a turn for the worse and the wind reared its ugly head to accompany the pounding rain. My feelings of negativity escalated. It hadn't stopped pouring since I arrived and I was feeling down-right fed up, which wasn't the fantastic start I had envisaged. Noticing my suicidal expression, Dad tried cheering me up.

"Let's go to Nerja and see if we can find some magazines you could work for," he said. Nerja is a popular tourist spot and where to go if you fancy ham egg and chips, or to hear kids throwing tantrums in the supermarket.

We found a couple of fat glossy freebies, but they looked a bit "more peas John?" and were aimed solely at the latter generation. Most of the articles focused on Inheritance Tax, Planning Your Funeral, and Where to Buy the Best Incontinence Pads. Despite the grim selection, I wrote a hard-hitting feature about the recent floods and emailed it to one. It took less than an hour to piece together and I included some terrific made-up quotes from affected English residents.

Later, in Torre del Mar, I picked up a smaller A5 sized magazine called *The Sentinel* and chuckled away at the Editor's quirky comments. It was a different concept, but worked extremely well.

"I love this magazine," said my Mum, grimacing at one of the jokes inside. "It's much more light-hearted than the others. Maybe you should get in touch with the Editor and see if you could work there."

"No way," I said. "It's too small to make enough money to pay me a wage."

However, I felt a spooky energy presence from *The Sentinel* magazine. At the time I had no idea why.

On my first Sunday in Spain the rain was still pouring so I spent the entire day indoors. The Spanish are still ten years behind England in the fact that no shops open on Sundays. The angry wind howled and whistled and the heavy rain splattered against the balcony doors. Rather than sit there staring into space, like a wizened old woman in a mental institute, I watched TV. Investing in Sky Television wasn't on the agenda for my parents, so that meant we were subjected to Spanish programmes. Flicking through the pathetic five channels, I longed for *BBC* or *Channel 4*. My choice of programmes was between a cheap version of *Wheel of Fortune*, a dubbed soap opera featuring the world's ugliest actors, the news, a cartoon, or the news. So the news it was, which was depressing, as I only managed to decipher five words throughout the whole slot, including 'Buenas noches'

A few days later the rain finally stopped, but the whole area looked a sodden mess. In Rincon de la Victoria, just twenty minutes from Torre del Mar, walls of properties had been completely washed away and in their place only a pile of rocks and a muddy sludge remained. Front gardens had literally vanished.

Despite the rain, my spirits rose when I saw my new apartment block. I was only able to view it from the outside, as I still hadn't signed the deeds, but it looked fresh and inviting. I was busting to venture inside, and wished my solicitors would get their finger out and do some work. Before moving to Spain I had heard about the "*mañana, mañana*" attitude which so many Spanish adopt.

"Don't expect anything to get done in a hurry," said a wise friend. "The Spanish aren't renowned for doing things quickly."

These words rung in my ears before a trip to the solicitors. It was my first meeting and I took an instant dislike to the pair. The man, who was the boss, had a head and face that reminded me of silly putty; I just wanted to mould the whole lot into something completely different. Then his peroxide blonde assistant strutted in as if she owned the firm, along with the rest of Spain and the world come to that. She wore killer high-heeled shoes, a barely-there skirt and a low-cut top that exaggerated her boobs. Her overpowering perfume tickled my nose and made me sneeze. As I left, my instincts warned me to fear the worst, and I anticipated utterly festering future news!

The sun finally popped her head out and luckily showed no signs of retreating. Taking advantage of the sudden good weather my parents and I visited

Algarrobo, where I had previously considered buying a pink five-bedroom town house for the same price as my one bed apartment. Algarrobo is divided into two parts; the costa (coast) and the pueblo (town and slightly inland). On this day we investigated the pueblo, a traditional white-washed village. The population was a mixture of hunched little old women with skin like crepe paper, and youngsters airing through the narrow streets astride their deafening mopeds. Algarrobo Pueblo is incredibly hilly with thick rigid steps leading to street after street of small terraced housing, occasionally interrupted by a smattering of tiny shops, not much larger than my fitted wardrobe.

"I'm glad I chose the apartment in El Morche," I said, watching an old lady struggling up steep hills with her shopping bags.

From the main residential area, we moved on to the new part of town, where there was a gorgeous park, adjacent to an outdoor swimming pool and three tennis courts.

Town visits with my parents were all very well, but pals were what I really craved. My "lack-of-friends" antennae was flashing brightly, and I prayed for a night at the local bars and nightclubs, having a laugh and being bombarded with ridiculous chat-up lines. As I heard the bars pumping-out songs until the early hours, I yearned to be amidst all the action, but going alone wasn't on the agenda. Some girls wouldn't mind entering a bar on their own, but I had always attached desperation and uncertainty to that. It was one thing being a loner and another having the world and his wife knowing about it.

One Saturday evening as I sat in front of a TV I couldn't understand, my phone beeped to an *sms* from a friend:

"Hi hon, me & the girls r clubbin 2nite on a biggy in Soho. Wish u were here xx".

The message made me feel so down in the dumps that instead of staying up thinking about how unappealing my life had become, I chose to have an early night. I woke up in a cold sweat and with soaking bed sheets, and eyed the clock; 4:30am. On a typical Saturday night in the UK, I would be waiting for a night bus packed with merry passengers talking nonsense, snoring or singing. There would be the lingering smell of chips and kebabs, the droning sound of laughter and chat, and that warm dancing feeling you get in your eyes after a few too many.

"Please God, find me some friends" I prayed.

Spanish Life

I took a step-up in the world upon opening a Spanish bank account. I didn't have much money to deposit, but it was a necessary formality when buying a property.

"You must fill in these forms" said the Manager, who had Ewok tendencies. I nearly fainted when I eyed the stack; there was an entire novel's worth.

"Tranquila" he said, as my face turned white. "I'll help you fill them in."

I half expected him to pull out a light-sabre and use his Ewok powers to complete them all at a single stroke. Actually, I simply had to sign each leaf, and I felt kind of famous afterwards.

"Anyone else for my autograph?" I thought of shouting across the eerily empty bank.

The Spanish banking system isn't favoured much by us Brits, as there are inexplicable charges, which aren't usually applicable in England. An annual commission is charged for so much as owning an account. There is a fee every time you debit a cheque, make a transfer and the rest. I wondered if breathing within the bank walls also incurred a fee.

Aside from the banking issues, the language barrier was becoming more evident. The cleaner who looked after my parents' apartment block, was very pleasant, and although we couldn't fight past the "hola, qué tal?" stage with her, we always made the effort to smile. She negotiated around the block daily, armed with a mop, an overflowing bucket and a filthy duster. One day, she appeared suddenly outside our front door, like something out of a horror movie, as we waited to catch the lift down. For decoration purposes my Mum had placed potted plants on every step leading from our floor up to the rooftop and the cleaner seemed vexed by their presence.

"Any idea what she's trying to say?" said my Dad wearing a puzzled expression and a deep frown.

"None at all" my Mum said, concentrating on the Spanish lady's lip movements.

"Me neither" I followed. "But her head looks like it's about to explode."

"I'm guessing she wants the plants moved inside" said my Father, beginning the chore.

Cleaner-lady shook her head hard, still talking incomprehensible banter. By this stage my Mum had picked out a few repeated words and after cheating with the phrase book, the message registered.

"Ah, she is saying that we should give the plants more water as they are withering" said my Mum, as if she had cracked a secret code.

All those days I had spent digesting Spanish books hadn't paid off, and what we thought was one very angry Spanish lady, transpired to be a thoroughly kind and thoughtful one!

Still officially friendless, I joined my parents again to explore another pueblo up the mountains, which is known in Spain as the *campo* (countryside). Many Brits pretend they speak Spanish by using the word *campo* in everyday speech, usually sandwiched between English words. Disappointingly, there wasn't much to see in Arenas. With temperatures hitting 90 degrees and many hills to combat, we soon felt our thirsts screaming to be quenched and, sod's law, there was no sign of a bar. The one glimpse of hope was totally shuttered up like *Cell Block H*, with a few crates of empty San Miguel bottles outside the door, as if saying 'Ha ha. You could have had me, but we've all gone'.

"Donde hay un restaurante?" I asked an old man, who had a face like a screwed up paper ball.

"Qué?" he bellowed. I guessed he was partially deaf so raised my voice. The words still didn't register.

"I've spent hours learning Spanish" I said to my parents. "Why is such a simple sentence so difficult to say?"

"You'd think he'd figure it out" said my Mum. "You can't be saying it so wrong."

After a further three times repeating the sentence, the old man finally realised we wanted a restaurant and repeated the word several times correctly, by accentuating the last but one syllable, "rrrestaur*aaaa*nte..." almost causing a landslide with the volume of his voice. I deciphered *iglesia,* the word for church, in his answer, so we headed for it. However, the so-called restaurant was nothing more than a dirty shed full of cigarette sucking, old men.

"I'd rather dig needles in my eyeballs without anaesthetic than join them" I said.

So after all that effort and still no drink, we hauled ourselves back to the car. We took the wrong route out of the village and had to do a three-point turn in a road barely wide enough for a go-kart. After many angry noises from the car and to the fascination and attempted arm-waving help from a bunch of locals, my Dad finally completed the manoeuvre with not a scratch to the body work. En-route to Torre del Mar , our mouths still screaming for liquid, we stopped at a roadside bar surrounded by nothing but dusty landscape, dying trees, towering mountains and winding roads.

"How on earth does this business survive?" I said. "It's a complete shambles."

It consisted of a ramshackle hut, filled with various home-made bottles of plonk and a bartender who looked like he belonged in a coffin. However the drinks were *campo* prices, so no complaints from my Dad, who paid the two-Euro bill with a smile.

It was Easter time, known as *Semana Santa* (Holy Week), and as the Spanish are a religious lot, it is celebrated hugely with processions. We went to Velez Málaga (five minutes inland from Torre del Mar) to watch it's version. Thousands of people strolled around aimlessly, stuffing their faces with the artery-blocking treats on sale in the surrounding booths. There were candy floss, sweets, crisps, nuts, popcorn, cakes and ice cream.

"No wonder child obesity is a growing problem" said my Mum as we observed a young, burly girl scoff a bag of sweets in record time. She had already devoured an ice cream, a box of popcorn and a doughnut. Surprisingly Easter Eggs weren't to be found anywhere. I later discovered that the Spanish don't celebrate Easter with chocolate eggs. In fact they don't exchange gifts at all.

The procession began slowly with hundreds of children parading the road, donning masks and carrying lit candles. Bizarrely, parents watching knew which was their own child, even though hooded garments covered each face. Every now and then we would see Señor or Señora Martín López waving frantically at a small masked human with a proud look upon their face. How they could tell that their son or daughter was under that particular mask (which I might add were all the same) is nothing short of a mystery. The parade of children was followed by seven or eight *tronos* (elaborate thrones adorned with religious statues and the like) held by struggling men, and seconded by steadily playing bands. Sadly, however, the buzzing heart-felt atmosphere was ruined by agonisingly long waits in between each statue's appearance. The older costume wearers and statue carriers wore long pointed triangular hats, perhaps to depict the executioners at the crucifixion of Jesus.

"Oooh, they look like the Klu Klux Klan" I said, as the fancily-clad men approached carrying a heavy statue of Jesus Christ.

"I'll bet that statue's heavy" said my Dad. "A few of them look like they're struggling."

In fact the statue carriers are so passionate about the Easter resurrection story that they often pay to fulfil the duty and suffer the following week with painful shoulders and neck-ache. The Spanish certainly take the entire Easter celebration a whole lot more seriously than we do in the UK, where chocolate eggs and bunny rabbits are all the hype.

Although slightly morbid, some of the statues looked amazing, draped with red and gold silk, and ablaze with hundreds of candles. The smell of incense brought the drama to life, as did the dried lavender strewn haphazardly across the road, like hundreds and thousands on a fairy cake. I took a trip down memory lane, to the annual church service I would usually attend on Good Friday, which gave me nightmares for the next three weeks. I much preferred this open-air, friendlier way of approaching a key day in Christianity. The story of Jesus being banged on to a cross with a hammer and nails and left to die an excruciating death, never failed to disturb me. The procession didn't end until gone two in the morning, but we left half an hour before full-time to seek the comfort of our beds.

Even though I had not yet signed the legal documents for my new apartment, I was invited to the first community meeting held at a venue in El Morche. My parents came too, just for the fun of it. The community deals with maintenance of the apartment block. It is the done thing in Spain to elect a president of the block to deal with any potential issues. Each month a payment is charged to all apartment owners to cover cleaning and repair works on the building. I expected a fairly low key, chilled out meeting. How wrong I was. The room was crammed full of passionate Spaniards, packed in like sardines, each with his or her own case to argue. The result was a confusion of raised voices, each trying to outdo the other, so that their point would be resolved first. It was no less than organised chaos. We three musketeers must have stuck out like sore thumbs, sat in utter disbelief, absorbing the rant these raving loons were producing.

"I wish they'd shut up" I said, placing my hands over my ears.

"Well they say the Spanish are the loudest country in Europe" said my Dad. "So there must be some truth in it."

The three Board Members looked far from impressed with the rebelling crowds. Every now and then the President, a man who looked like a Spanish version of Santa Claus, hammered his gavel on the table in a bout of frustration, craving silence.

Dolores, who sold me the apartment, joined us to decipher the day's proceedings. Dolores is a serious looking forty-something lady, who uses the wrong shade of hair dye. She rarely smiles, but speaks fairly good English. She looks like the 'mumsy' type and I wouldn't be surprised if she likes dogs. Estate agents play a large role when it comes to selling property to clients, generally seeing you right through to the (often bitter) end.

The Santa Claus double was turning a deep shade of crimson, a similar colour to Rudolph's nose. After his next outburst I very nearly called an ambulance. The frustration had built up to such a degree that a sudden head-shaking anger surge erupted from his persona, which could have brought on a heart attack.

"Silencio," he yelled. His plan worked. The energetic performance shut up the raging masses. The noise came to an abrupt halt and silence stepped in. Santa Claus's right hand lady, who looked like she would rather be held at gun point than sat in the room for a minute longer, adjusted her specs and began to speak. Intermittently, Dolores whispered a vague translation in my ear. Her breath smelt like dog dung. All manner of issues were raised, from the colour of the balcony awnings, to the amount each apartment would pay per month, according to its size in square metres. My payment worked out to thirty-five Euros per month, which was cheap considering that in the UK I paid sixty pounds a month for the corridors to be vacuumed once a week.

I noticed from the community meeting handout that all the Spanish had two surnames.

"One is the Dad's name and the other the Mum's," said Dolores. "When a baby is born they take one of each." I was glad I only had one surname. Completing forms would take so much longer otherwise.

"How about if I marry a Spanish man?" I said. "Do I gain another surname, or keep just the one?"

"Just your original. Not like in England where you have to take the man's."

My name had a nice ring to it and I had always hated the thought of marrying a Mr Bogg or a Mr Pratt. So at least I had learnt one worthwhile thing from this meeting. I had to marry a Spanish chap!

Two hours and two pain-killers later we were only half-way through the agenda and my headache was nearing migraine stage, so I mouthed a swift goodbye to Dolores and slipped out the door, inhaling a lungful of fresh air.

Easter Sunday was another beautifully sunny day on the Costa del Sol so we spent the afternoon in Torremolinos, which is a stone's throw from Málaga airport and the resort where stereotypical sunburnt British tourists hang out. You know the kind I mean. The sort of cringe-worthy clan who read The Sun, eat fry-ups daily and down as much draught beer as they can possibly cram into their rotting guts. They have names like Wayne and Tracey and swear at their children so that they become miniature versions of them. The teenagers strut around pushing prams and wearing fake Burberry and gold rope chains; the Mums have bleach blonde hair and leathery fake tans, and the Dads have skinheads and are decorated from head to toe in hideous tattoos. All smoke like chimneys and use the F word too much.

"Trace, Trace," one shouted from the other side of the road. "Get me a pint will you love, I just got to change Tyler. He's being a right fucking pain in the butt today. There's no fucking way I'm having any more little shits like him."

"Lovely" I thought, as I watched her cart her child to the toilets.

I didn't like the Brit-infested feel of Torremolinos, nor the numerous steps which made the journey down to the beach tortuous.

"So would you like to live here?" asked my Dad.

"Definitely not," I said. "It's OK for a flying visit, but that's all. Give me Torre del Mar any day."

Torre del Mar appealed far more than Torremolinos, due to the key fact that it was still predominately Spanish. The Brits had not yet invaded, however I knew in the future that would be inevitable. Dolores had told me that within the last ten years the Axarquia area had changed enormously in terms of infrastructure, housing and tourism. Another decade would see yet more changes, almost guaranteed. I wanted to meet British people more than anything, to make some friends, but I was after a certain kind, certainly not of the calibre mentioned above.

I spent the rest of the day lounging around, which was the story of my life lately. The three and a half weeks I had spent living at my Mum and Dad's were taking their toll. I missed my independence and the company of young people. I contemplated returning to England, where I felt confident approaching a man at the bar, or sharing a chin-wag with a complete stranger. Here in Spain that confidence was hugely lacking. My row-ometer, which hovered at a safe two when I first arrived in Spain, was now touching five and my parents were the unlucky duo on the receiving end of my foul mood. The best way of dealing with this was to pretend my parents weren't actually there and that I was the only person in the room.

"What's the matter?" asked my Mum over lunch. "You've been as miserable as sin all day."

I physically couldn't answer. The words wouldn't rise to leave my mouth. I wanted to say, "What do you mean, what's the matter? I hate living here, where I have no job, no friends and no purpose. I wish I had never stepped foot on the plane and had stayed in England." But I was speechless. So this is what they meant by clinical depression. Now I knew. Instead of answering a question to which the answer seemed ridiculously obvious, I continued eating my cheese sandwich and stared out to sea, wishing I had been born a dolphin, a shark, a rat, anything but a human. It was almost as if my questioning Mum wasn't even on the same planet.

"Keidi?" she probed, now sounding worried.

"Nothing," I said, without breaking down into tears. I could feel my eyes welling up, so I ran to my room for a much-needed cry.

As I sat on my bed, surrounded by soggy tissues, I reflected on my situation and realised that it had all come about as a result of my own doing. It was me who decided to buy a place in Spain, me who had chosen to leave my comfy seat in the UK and up sticks to a new country and a new life. I had no one to blame apart from myself. "If only I had more self confidence" I thought. "Then I could remedy the situation". If I was like other 'normal' twenty-something girls, by this time I would have made some friends, found a job (doing anything) and perhaps even have met a man, but I just could not summon up the drive to make things happen. It was all too overwhelming for little old me. I spared a thought for my parents, who went out of their way to help and reassure me. I knew my miserable mood was affecting them too. They hated seeing their daughter, who was once an abundance of fun and energy, so depressed and emotional. I wanted to feel good again, not only for me, but also for them.

That evening, in a desperate bid to cheer me up, my parents took me to a bar, which was holding a pool tournament. There were quite a few English people meandering but as usual they mostly hovered in the fifty-plus age range. Spaniards dominated the bar, which was OK considering we were in Spain. The younger ones started from the age of fifteen, using the area as some kind of youth club, complete with cans of pop, potato chips, and bubble gum. My eyes almost burst out their sockets when I saw two English girls enter the bar, followed by their parents. Their blonde hair and fair skin gave away their British nationality and they looked more or less my age. Plus I saw no signs of Burberry, prams, or gold chunky jewellery.

"Go and speak to them," said my Dad. "This could be your chance to make some friends." He was trying to help as much as he possibly could, God bless. I pictured him in a comic. "Is it a bird, is it a plane? No it's Super-Dad…!"

Usually I would have had the confidence to approach the girls, but something stopped me. A wasted opportunity had fled into the past, now too late to alter. At least I now knew young English people existed in Spain. It was just a case of hunting them down.

Time flew by and I had forgotten my sense of self and purpose. For a while I was trapped in a state of deep depression and anxiety. I began to think I had made a huge mistake. I didn't seem to be having much luck with anything. Perhaps I had taken the wrong turning on the path life had marked out for me and someone up above was telling me to turn back and correct it.

Firstly, I still hadn't received the keys to my apartment. This major worry seemed to be dragging on and on and there wasn't an end in sight to the daily ritual of phoning the solicitors, or calling in to demand meetings with The Fat Controller or Ms Own the World. Each time I saw her she looked even more venomous than the last. Her clothes became skimpier and tartier and her make up was another layer thicker. I imagined her hacking it off with a chisel before bedtime. This firm of clowns was now charging me an extra thousand Euros because the sale had taken so long to go through. As if it was my fault. Perhaps if they had got off their ample backsides towards the beginning and actually done some work we wouldn't be in this position. Most days I felt like screaming, bashing walls and displaying the antics of an insane woman who belonged in an asylum. The solicitors said that the signing, which was meant to have happened three months ago, wouldn't occur until the following week at the earliest.

Secondly, I still didn't have a job and that side of the coin was looking far from promising. There were bar jobs a-plenty, but I refused to earn money pulling pints. Mr Money still hadn't contacted me about the job offer in Marbella, so my mind was turning to new ways of earning a living.

Thirdly, I still hadn't met any people my own age, who I would even consider good friends. The few I had met were either fugitives on the run from violent offences, in hiding from equally violent debt collectors, or drugged up to their eyeballs.

To top this misery off, my parents announced they were returning to the UK for a holiday, so I was faced with the prospect of staying all alone with no-one to talk to apart from me, myself and I. Nothing smelt of roses, more like decaying horse manure. I dreamt my luck would change direction and everything would start going right. I have always believed that throughout the long slog called life one must experience good and bad spells. You must muscle through the bad spells, in order to be rewarded with the good. I felt like screaming up to the high heavens:

"Haven't I had enough bad? Where's my good?"

Maybe the angels had forgotten about my good slice. Perhaps it was bad pie all the way from now on.

A week later I finally saw inside my apartment for the first time. As the car pulled up outside a brand new block, my stomach made the grumbling noise it usually makes when I am feeling nervous but excited. This was one of those milestone days for me. The day when I could see my home in which I would live as soon as humanely possible. The home into which I could invite friends (when I made some) and in which I could slob around stark naked if I chose. My home to do with what I wanted. Dolores the estate agent let us in. The moment I had been waiting for since arriving in Spain. My heart was beating fast, the door swung open and...

"Oh my God!"

The first sight that met my eyes was...wait for it... a black wall. My hall wall smothered in mould and ugly yellow specks. Not a pleasant sight and totally unexpected. I gazed at Dolores who shrugged her shoulders with a look which said, "well what's the problem, it's only a mouldy wall. This is Spain, they come as standard here." I felt like bawling on the spot. An inspection of the other rooms resulted in more disappointment. There were rotten door frames, doors that wouldn't shut, crumbling paint work, an insect nest in the bottom of the wardrobe. The list continued. Dolores made a phone call.

"It seems the apartment above flooded," she said. "That's the reason for the dampness. I'll speak to the builders to see if they can fix the problems."

All this, and just when I thought things couldn't possibly get any worse. I left El Morche that day feeling totally dejected and I wouldn't have cared if I had dropped stone cold dead on the spot.

Later I cheered up a notch at the news that my best chum Liz was coming to visit when my parents returned to the UK.

"It'll be so cool having someone to explore the night clubs with," I told her down the phone. I had a month and a half of missed night life to make up for in seven days. At last, something worth living for!

Moving Forward

My stomach wouldn't stop dancing, as I was meeting Mr Money about the world's longest job vacancy, *at last*! I was exuding excitement at the thought that my unemployment agony might be over by lunch time, but I desperately tried to retain a cool exterior. I pictured myself as a high profile magazine editor flitting between celebrity interviews, free lunches and designer shops. A chic Londoner living it up in the rich area of the Costa del Sol, with a job others would envy. Wealthy men. Yachts. Ferraris. Wealthy men. Yachts. Ferraris. Wealthy men. Yachts. Ferraris. The three words bounced around my head, luring me to a new and pretentious life, like a conveyor belt on a game show, showing what I could win, if my luck was ripe.

I wondered what it would be like to have cash to splash; enough money to buy what I wanted, when I wanted, without having to worry about covering the rent each month. Mr Money told me I had the job in February and I assumed he had asked me to journey all the way to Marbella, to reveal a starting date. Why else?

My Dad drove the hour and a half slog. My head was like a washing machine, churning around at speed, while pondering over all the possibilities of the forthcoming meeting.

We had agreed to meet outside a café, beneath his office. He emerged out of a random door with a folder under his arm. He looked 'wrong'. His eyes were bloodshot and baggy, his skin was dull and grey. If he was a piece of fruit one would have speculated that he was going off.

"Follow me" he said, leading me up some steps to his office.

There were two rooms overlooking a busy main road. I immediately observed that there was no furniture, no computer desks and no phones. No photocopier, no paper clip chains, no naked women calendars, nor any other tell tale 'we work from here' signs. Just one empty office, which clearly needed fitting.

"Right" I said. "So when are you proposing to use this office as an, errm, office?"

"That's what I wanted to talk to you about," said Mr Money with a guilty glint in his flagging eye. "You see, we aren't quite ready to roll yet. Things are taking longer than we imagined, you know, red tape and all that." He laughed nervously and unduly.

I must have guessed what was coming next and he must have seen the disappointment flood my face.

"Look, Keidi, I'm sorry. I really want you to work on the magazine. I think you're perfect for the position, but not quite yet. Can you hang in there for another couple of months? I'll call you as soon as the circumstances change. Mark my words."

I pictured myself as a puppet on strings, with Mr Money towering over me, moving me how he wanted, when he wanted and I didn't like it. The idea of 'hanging on' for something, which would probably never happen, didn't appeal. This game had been played for far too long and I was losing. I had just slid down the longest snake on the board, back to square one. My life would now entail seeking the ladder so I could climb back up to the top. I was sick to death of all the false promises of calls and starting dates, physically exhausted. I shook my head in disbelief.

"You mean I've come here today, all this way, just so you can tell me that you're not quite ready to take me on?" I stammered. His guilty glint turned guiltier.

"Yeah," he said. "I thought it'd be better to tell you to your face, rather than on the phone."

His logic seemed about as sane as some of George Bush's policies. I wanted to grab him round the neck and squeeze hard. I wanted to pull his hair out, hit him and scream obscenities, but without wanting to cause a scene, I said an abrupt "Goodbye" slammed the door deliberately hard and left the office to seek my parents, who were sitting in the café below.

"So how did it go? They asked in unison.

I ended the day feeling so depressed that if I were Sleeping Beauty I would have made sure there was a prince-trap outside my door before bedtime. The light, to which I had been attracted, like a moth to a bulb, had suddenly gone out. This was the day I realised I may have no other option than to return to the country I so desperately yearned to escape from. Reality had hit home and the thought of returning there was about as treacherous as having a travelling companion with a serious case of BO.

The next day there was an outbreak of ladybirds on my parents' balcony. The entire awning was covered with the red and black spotted insects. I took the ladybirds as another sign from God. So far I had experienced flash floods, dashed hopes, mouldy walls, false job offers and now a plague! I wondered what was coming next. The only light I could focus on was my friend's visit, which was fast approaching.

In the meantime, something remarkable, timely and utterly hilarious happened out the blue. I was reading the May issue of the magazine to which I had e-mailed my flood story a few weeks ago, when I stumbled across a chunk in one of the features that sounded remarkably familiar, a quote from a Patricia Parker. I soon realised that this quote formed part of my article, which I e-mailed to the Editor, so he could consider me for a full-time position. It was not an invitation to print my work, just a sample of my writing. Patricia Parker didn't even exist in Rincon. I made her and the quote up! 'If he uses half my stories he has to pay me for them,' I thought. 'And if he uses half my stories he must like them, so he can take me on as a writer.' That was more like it. I suddenly switched into full beam of my favourite personality trait. I imagined myself as a female version of Arnold Schwarzenegger in The Terminator, but I was Keidi Keating and I was The Determinator. Nothing was going to slip past me, I was made of steel. I rang the magazine office and asked to talk to the Editor.

"Speaking," answered a kind sounding chappy. "How can I help?"

"My name's Keidi Keating," I said. "I emailed you a story about the floods in Rincon recently and it seems you have printed part of it in your magazine."

"Yes," said the Editor. "Thanks for those brilliant quotes, very forward thinking of you. My staff never think like that. You were a reporter in England, right?"

I felt like he was shunning the issue, so twisted the conversation to put it back on track, my track.

"Spot on," I said. "So how much do I get paid for that story then?"

"Well we normally pay seventy Euros for a complete feature with photos, so how does twenty-five Euros sound?"

It sounded pathetic, like the dregs of an old man's pint, or the Chinese left-overs you wouldn't even feed a starving dog for fear of killing it. Nonetheless, I gratefully accepted. At the end of the day this man was a boss and bosses need to be sucked-up to. It goes with the territory.

"Are there any full time positions available on your magazine?" I asked.

"Not right now, but one may come up in the future," he said. "In the meantime I can offer you freelance work at the usual going rate."

At last, my brain was back in use. After six weeks of stand by I could finally pass Go. Was life improving? Had I hit rock bottom? Was the only way from up from now on? Had I found the ladder at long last? The printed magazine story started my ball rolling and gave me hope, a light at the end of tunnel. I just had to work at it. Things don't come to those that sit and wait. You have to make your own opportunities, your own life, pave your own future. I had seen sense, thank the high heavens.

That afternoon, Dolores called.

"The work on your apartment will be completed tomorrow," she said. "You can come and see it and then sign at the notary office the day after."

"The planets are moving in Scorpio's favour at long last"' I thought. Mystic Meg high five!

I arrived expecting to see all the work completed. However, my hopes were dashed when I discovered none of it had even been started. The mouldy wall was as rotten as before. Dolores had stupidly presumed that introducing me to the builder who would be carrying out the work would reassure me to sign at the notary office. That afternoon a visit to the solicitors transpired to be a stressful experience as many high-pressure phone calls were made. The promoter, responsible for managing the sale of the apartments, finally agreed that if all the work was not complete within ten days of the signing, they would pay me to have the work completed by somebody else.

Lunchtime came and my Dad returned from the local bar with news. Bad news.

"That chap who runs the Sentinel Magazine is in hospital," he said. "No one knows what's wrong with him, but apparently he's really sick."

The Sentinel was the A5 magazine which we all enjoyed reading. It was suggested that I could help prepare the next issue if they needed me. At the time I didn't know it, but this news would play a significant role regarding my future in Spain.

Seven weeks had crawled by since I arrived in Spain. Seven weeks ago I thought I would sign for my apartment within a mere few days. After this seven weeks of worrying, wondering and wailing, Judgement Day had arrived. The day of reckoning. The day of signing. I awoke with butterflies and that feeling I often encounter when I anticipate that the day isn't going to run smoothly. The Notary office was exceedingly busy, packed with soon to be home-owners, just as anxious as me. Dolores and the promoters were smiles a-plenty upon my arrival, but that was just a front.

"Right, first things first," I said. "Where's the document that the promoters agreed to sign yesterday?"

Dolores looked embarrassed.

"Oh, they decided that they don't want to sign it after all," she said. My stomach performed a series of energetic somersaults. What planet did they think I was from? Zog?

"Well I'm not signing the deeds for the apartment until that document has been signed by the promoters" I said, voice raised.

The trio's smiles turned to scowls and initially they refused. I was feeling incredibly stubborn, so stood my ground. I felt like saying, "You are the weakest link. Goodbye," coupled with an Anne Robinson wink. I knew they would sign the document. They had travelled all the way from Madrid so to return with no money would be ludicrous. If they were so confident that my mouldy wall issue would be solved within ten days, I didn't see why it was such a big deal to sign. Dolores failed to see my point of view. She said the work was going to be complete that day, but she had said the same on three days previously, to no avail. After many serious phone calls and a spate of secret liaisons, finally, one hour and one signed document later we were called to sign-over a mouldy apartment to little old me.

The buying process here in Spain is not at all civilised like it is in England. Here everyone involved in the sale, including buyer(s), seller(s), estate agents, promoters and bank manager (if there's a mortgage involved) must congregate in a small room to witness the signing and hand-over of the keys. The stony-faced notary man glanced over the necessary documents with a sullen expression.

"Me deja su pasaporte?" he asked, glancing in my direction.

My heart dropped to my ankles and I gulped like a bullfrog. Passport? No one told me I needed to bring my passport. I looked from the solicitor to the bank manager to the estate agent, praying that one of them would pluck it from thin air and say "Here it is." But they didn't.

Instead they returned my glares with anxious undertones, rolling their eyes to the ceiling when they gathered I didn't have it. The notary man looked agitated, glaring at his watch as if time were gold. There was no way we were going to reach that stage and not sign, so he agreed we could resume in 15 minutes, once I had run home and returned with my passport. I ran like Forest Gump. "Run Keidi run," I heard in the defined American accent, as my legs pumped out energy faster than a solar panel. I returned to the notary office and burst into the room with passport held high. I felt like an Olympic sprinter with the trophy. An Olympic winner, sweating like a pig in a wig and breathing like a woman in labour. After the passport check, which took three seconds and seemed like such a triviality after that mammoth run, it was time to prepare the 'Black Money.'

This sounds like a fatal disease, which you can catch from touching the same money as an infected person, but in fact Black Money means the illegal part; the part that the notary man refuses to be associated with, so leaves the room as if oblivious. In his absence the outstanding cash is passed across the table and when he reckons the process is complete Notary Man re-enters the room to continue. Signing was over in five minutes flat and the seven weeks of build up suddenly seemed distant and insignificant. After all the trauma I received nothing more than a new set of keys.

My friend Liz arrived that morning so we collected her before driving straight to my new apartment. I wanted to check that my keys worked! On the way we hedged our bets on whether the mould and other problems would be sorted. Imagine my pleasant surprise when the door swung open and a brilliant white wall met my eye! Fortunately, the builders had got their paintbrushes out.

"Let me give you a tour," I told my friend, like a child with a new toy. When I had shown her all four rooms and given her a running commentary of what furniture would live where, I said "adiós" to my new apartment. I knew I wouldn't see it again until my parents had returned from their holiday to England. This holiday was a mutual necessity for both parties. My row-ometer had hit five and six more and more, lately, and I was finding my parents' annoying nit-picking habits highly distressing. In the same way, they must have viewed my selfish brat tendencies as really unwelcome. I was glad to see the back of them for a week and I knew the feeling was mutual. In their place I was enthralled to see my best friend Liz, who I would share much fun with throughout the week.

Liz was my closest friend throughout secondary school. I always knew we would keep in touch throughout life. We had a mutual understanding of each other, perhaps because we were born a mere eight days apart. Physically we are certainly not peas in a pod. Liz is shorter than I, with short blonde hair and large green eyes. She is funny and intelligent and often described as an enigma.

On her first night we fancied man action so hit the sea-front bars, where four or five stand in a row. We chose a mysteriously empty *live music bar* and plotted at a table inside with double Southern Comforts. Gradually the bar began to fill. We performed a three hundred and sixty degree scan and noticed that all the tables were suddenly occupied. A young unattractive man with an unshaven face and spectacles dragged a microphone on to the stage, testing for sound quality. He looked like an older version of the Milky Bar kid, but unfortunately without the free chocolate bars. Our table choice couldn't have been worse if we had tried. We were at the table closest to the stage and this was comedy night.

"Oh my God," Liz said with a worried look. "This could be bad news. If comedy nights are anything like those in London, the comedian always targets the people sitting in the front row."

"Plus we won't understand any of the jokes," I said. "Come on let's leave now."

Too late! The comedian's performance had started and all attention was now fixed on the Milky Bar Kid. If we left we would run an even higher risk of suffering extreme embarrassment. Instead we downed the remains of our drinks and sat tight. Every thirty seconds, the entire bar would burst into uncontrollable fits of laughter. Everyone except for us. It got to the stage where we were the only two laughing when nothing funny had been said. We had reverted to schoolgirl days and laughed more at the awkward situation we found ourselves in than anything else. Thankfully Milky Bar Kid didn't veer down the 'rip it out of your audience' path so we were safe, but uncertain. At half time we paid the bill and pelted to the bar next door.

"How about going out in Nerja tonight?" I suggested over a bowl of muesli the next morning. "The night-life is meant to be better there."

We spent the rest of the day boosting our tans on the beach, deciding what to wear and wondering if there would be any fit men to chat up. Imagine our disappointment when we arrived to an empty town. I felt like shouting at the top of my lungs: "Where is everrrrrrrrrybodddddddddy?" We wondered whether everyone else knew something we didn't. Was Nerja about to be attacked with nuclear missiles, meteorites, or invaded by little green men with too many eyes? A lone man appeared from around a corner and noticed our baffled faces.

"If you're wondering why it's so dead here, everyone's at the Nerja Feria," he said. "It's held on the outskirts of town, near Maro."

We didn't fancy the feria so took a taxi back to Torre, driven by the cabby from hell, who had seemingly smoked too much wacky backy. His head was rolling on his neck, his eyes were rolling in his head, his car was rolling all over the road and we were rolling all over the back seat. As I watched the speedo hit a hundred and seventy kph I fastened my seatbelt and said a short prayer. We spent the night in Torre del Mar, irritating Spanish ladies with our natural charm and beauty, and attracting the interest of many Spanish men, who hovered around us like flies.

My parents returned to Spain a week later and Liz went back to England. I felt very sad as I had enjoyed Liz's company and had regained some form of independence, with my parents away.

A few days later my Dad had some more news.

"*The Sentinel* man, Colin, has died from Leukaemia. He was only forty-six you know?"

"That's terrible" I said. "So young, and it all happened so quickly. It was only a week ago you told me he was in hospital."

"Yeah, everyone's in shock" he said. "It just shows you, we never know what life's gonna throw our way next."

Colin was bitten by a snake while walking his dog in the countryside and rushed to hospital in case of blood poisoning. Standard blood tests revealed the cancer. After hearing the awful news, he lasted just one week.

"Anyway I know it's not the best circumstances, but it could be an opening for you" followed my Dad.

"What do you mean?"

"Well you could carry on *The Sentinel*. You'll have to speak to Colin's father of course, to make sure that's OK I mean, maybe now isn't the right time, but in a few weeks perhaps. "

The Lord moves in mysterious ways and my father was right. This terrible tragedy could be my light. This man's awful death could bring me a new life. Maybe all that bad karma I had experienced of late was finally changing direction. I thought about how I would broach the subject when talking to Colin's father.

"Hi there, I'm Keidi. My Dad's the guy who drinks in the bar sometimes with you. Sorry to hear about your son's death. Oh and can I have his job by the way?"

Tact certainly wasn't my strong point.

Firsts

My new apartment block is called Edificio Luna, which translates as the 'moon building', perhaps because it is an absurd circular shape. My apartment is on the first floor, but because it was built on a hill, to reach it there are steps up, down, up again, then down again. I went there to off-load my worldly possessions, which had become part of my parents' furniture.

Edificio Luna is only five storeys high and as such, appears fairly modern and contemporary. It is tri-colour, with red bricks at the base, topped with a yellow painted section, then a white area. It reminds me of a fancy cake my Nan used to bake. Inside it is light and spacious. A wide corridor and steps led to a small swimming pool, nestled in the middle of all the apartments.

Entering on the right is a bathroom with dark red flooring and white wall tiles. There is a bathtub with shower, sink, loo and a bidet. Opposite the bathroom is the kitchen, which at the time was just an empty space, still to be fitted. Along the hall is the living room with marble floors. I had pine furniture, strategically placed around the edge, to make the most of the space. I had a coffee table, fold out dining table and chairs, computer desk, sofa bed, two wall units and a TV stand. Lastly the bedroom, where there was nothing but my double bed and a fitted wardrobe. I still had lights to fit in all rooms and had my boxes to sort through, but I had more-or-less everything needed to live in comfort. Once the water and electricity were connected and a kitchen was fitted, I could officially move in.

I had heard a number of horror stories about people waiting months for their electricity to be connected, so I was expecting the worst.

"We may as well give it a clean while we're here" said my Mum, eyeing the dust and grime with horror.

"The builders haven't left it in a very good condition."

She was right. There was plaster splattered on the doors and frames, paint drips on the skirting boards and dusty floors. The cleaning operation took a good few hours, as we scrubbed, mopped, polished and wiped.

"It'll have to do for now" said my Mum, wiping sweat from her brow. "You can give it another go over when you move in."

We stood on the balcony to cool down. My outlook wasn't quite sea-view, but rather main road. I watched the cars and lorries racing past, wishing I was rich and could afford something more glamorous.

El Morche is a small town in comparison to others along the Costa del Sol. There was an abundance of construction work taking place. Poky old-style houses were being ripped down and replaced with brand new apartment blocks. In the car on the way back I counted twenty-seven cranes. Business-wise there were just a few cafes, bars and estate agents. I could see that changing as more people moved in. The real beauty of the town is the beach. It is one of the only sandy beaches along this stretch of the coast and the sea is shallow for a long way out. It had a wild, un-used and less touristy feel about it than other beaches in the area. I had a feeling that El Morche would really take off in the future and I wanted to be there when it did.

That evening my Mum received a phone call from my older sister Kami, who, along with my two older brothers, still lived in England. When she hung up she looked like a cat who had swiped a full saucer of cream.

"Come on…what's the news?"

She displayed that knowing grin on her face, which I can frequently read.

"Ah, I know, she's pregnant?"

It wasn't hard to fathom. She had been living with her boyfriend for eight years and they showed no signs of splitting up. Plus she had started to collect Baby Magazines, a sure sign of looming motherhood. To begin with my Mum was all smiles, but within fifteen minutes she became withdrawn and a little sad. As a childminder for the last fifteen years and a lover of little ones, it had suddenly sunk in that she wouldn't see much of her first grandchild. The moment she moved to Spain, her oldest daughter revealed she was expecting. I suspect she found it unfair.

"She's going to be born on November the sixth" I told my parents later that night. I had no idea where the date had come from.

"How do you know she'll have a girl?" said my Dad. "Kami might have a boy."

"No a girl" I said. "Born on the sixth of November, you'll see."

"The baby isn't due till the seventeenth" said my Mum "And usually a first child is late, not early."

I wasn't deterred.

"Well let's just wait and see," I said with a smile, which spoke volumes. I had the knack of successfully predicting events before they happened and had always believed I was slightly psychic.

The next day we awoke early for *Mijas International Day*. The glossy magazine in Nerja had asked me to write a feature about it. My first commissioned story in Spain, so at last I could put my reporter's hat back on and give my life a sense of purpose again.

Mijas is located past Torremolinos, in the 'English' area of the Costa del Sol, west of Málaga. We drove up a huge mountain to reach the pueblo. Fortunately, as opposed to Mijas Costa, the pueblo is still predominately Spanish, but the English are slowly discovering the area. The beautiful white washed town stands at four hundred and twenty-eight metres above sea level and it boasts cobbled streets and traditional Spanish features. Craft shops sell hand-made pottery and beautiful paintings by talented artists. On this day, there were stalls, shows and people a-plenty. The event began with a huge parade, in which children from across the globe gathered to represent their country. They donned traditional costume, marching and dancing to the national song. Spectators tapped their feet and clapped their hands in time to the addictive beat of drummers and bass players.

My Dad was photographer, and as I observed and absorbed the energetic activity, he performed his magic with the camera, stooping, towering and squirrelling when necessary. Later, we walked around the stalls, of which one was dedicated to each country represented. At lunch-time there was a chance to taste foods from across the world, with each stall serving a selection of their country's delicacies to passers by. That evening an outdoor concert was performed, which set the crowds off dancing, drinking and letting down their hair. There was a great sense of united spirit in Mijas and it was a real pleasure to be part of it. My sense of well being, which had been drastically lapsing, was re-instated and it felt wonderful. The finale firework display was amazing and ended a perfect day just perfectly…!

As my creative juices were flowing, I had the writing bug again, and feeling on top form I emailed a large glossy magazine in England asking if I could write some features for them. Self-belief is an important tool and right then I was literally oozing it. I emailed a few initial ideas, including my lurid property purchasing experience. At the same time, my parents droned on at me like a broken record to call Colin's dad about continuing to produce the magazine, but I had no idea what to say and more importantly how to say it.

"I can't" I told my Dad. "But you can call him for me if you want."

I was using the situation to my advantage. I knew my parents wanted me to stay in Spain and if there was any whiff of a chance they would go out of their way to help. As predicted, my Dad picked up the phone.

"Hi, it's Pat here, who drinks with you sometimes in Torre. I'm ever so sorry about your son's death. Look my daughter Keidi is a journalist so if you say it's OK, she would like to continue *The Sentinel*. Yeah. Really? OK, well thanks very much. Oh, right. I'll let her know. Thanks again. Bye."

Colin's father said he didn't mind me continuing to produce *The Sentinel*, but he knew nothing, so couldn't help me at all. Apparently all the information and past documents were stored on Colin's computer and no one could access it – it wasn't as if we could ring heaven to find out what the password was. I imagined the conversation: Ring, ring. Ring, ring:

"Hello. You're through to the angel hotline. How can I help?"

"A Colin Checkley entered heaven recently and I need to have a word with him."

"Hold the line please I will need to check the system." (a pause) "It seems that Mr Checkley hasn't yet arrived. He's on the waiting list, but entry can take anything up to one week. Rest assured that he's on his way."

Back to the real world and with all hopes dashed of finding out even an ounce of information about *The Sentinel*, it was time to put my detective hat on. I went to talk to Colin's best friend Joe, who ran a bar in Torre del Mar, to see if he could reveal some further clues about *The Sentinel*. Joe was an odd-ball, who scared off potential customers with his sullen looks and harsh words. Colin's sudden death had dragged Joe's mood even further into the realms of misery land.

"So you want to carry on with *The Sentinel*" said Joe glaring through soul-less eyes, which told me they had given up on life. "Well, let me tell you now, you'll have a hard task doing that. Everyone loves the way Colin writes you know. It'll take something to match it. Spain isn't an easy country to live and work in. I know that much. First hand experience. Bloody fed up of running this place I am, been here five years now would you believe? Five years," he repeated, shaking his head and snorting like a pot-bellied pig.

In my experience the best way to deal with negative people is to battle them with a flurry of positive words. It works wonders in dispelling any negative vibes. I picture my positive army on horseback with weapons in hand. I then picture the opposing side (the negative army) with just a few injured men, no horses and a lack of weapons. The battle begins and the positive army thrashes the negative army; wins hands down. All I can see in my head at that point is a sea of little plus signs. Victory.

"I have a great feeling that if I continue with *The Sentinel* magazine it will do really well," I said. "I'm young and I have the energy to make it work. I would really appreciate it if you could help with a few things though…"

It was like squeezing blood out of a stone, but eventually Joe told me where Colin had his magazines printed. Fortunately it was located only a two-minute walk from my parent's apartment.

In the meantime my parents and I started Spanish lessons, as we realised that in order to get anywhere, learning the language was essential. The teacher was a lovely little lady called Maria, who was patient, clear speaking and boasted a calm aura. Maria had this wonderful knack of putting pupils at ease and not making us feel stupid when we couldn't answer her questions. Trouble was, the lesson agenda consisted of the basic beginners content that I taught myself on the daily train journeys home from London the year before, including phrases such as 'I live in…' and 'my name is…'. Mum and I understood practically every word Maria said, reflecting that all the time spent memorising Spanish children's books had paid off. My poor Dad, who only knew five or six essential words, including *gracias, hola* and not surprisingly *cerveza* (beer), struggled a tad. Fortunately for him, there were just the three of us in the class, retaining his embarrassment levels to a safe minimum. The classes only lasted three months and then my Mum and I decided we would be better off teaching ourselves. I had hoped I might meet some young English people at the Spanish lessons, whom I could adopt as friends, but my luck was out.

These days, my parents had a better social life than me and that was rather worrying. One day two of their chums, Doug and Lynne, who lived in a tiny village high in the hills, invited us to a barbecue.

"Bring your daughter as well, won't you" said Doug on the blower to my Dad.

As it transpired, Doug and Lynne had a daughter called Sarah, about my age, who happened to be visiting them on the afternoon of the barbecue. Sarah was a nanny in the UK and enjoyed long holidays, which she spent in Spain with her parents. She had long silky smooth hair, and an angelic, pretty face.

"I might be moving here permanently in a couple of months" she said, tossing her hair from her model-like complexion. She went on to say that her nanny job was coming to an end and that she had been offered a position in an international school in Málaga.

"When I'm next over, we could meet up for a drink" she said.

"Cool" I said. "That would be fantastic." Finally I had caught my first whiff of a real friend.

Later I excitedly read an e-mail from *Viva España*, the magazine I approached regarding writing features for them. They asked me to write an account about a young person's property purchasing experiences, for a very welcome three hundred pounds. I started it that evening. It felt so therapeutic to become lost in a maze of words again. Writing is a hypnotic pastime for me. My mind becomes redundant to any outside delusions. It's the only time it doesn't worry excessively, wander dangerously or reflect harmfully. Some people choose drinking to excess in order to relax, others work out in the gym, or snort illegal substances, but my vice is simply writing. Give me a pen and paper, or a computer with keyboard and I'm as happy as a pig in mud. I finished the feature within a couple of hours and felt mighty pleased with the result. I hoped the editor would think likewise.

Nevertheless, freelancing was never going to be a permanent career move. What I really needed was my own business and *The Sentinel* magazine had been handed to me on a plate. I prepared a visit to the printers, to find out if producing it would make a satisfactory income. Before leaving, I spent some time with the dictionary to familiarise myself with the words and phrases which I was likely to encounter.

Magazine: *Revista*

Pages: *Páginas*

Colour: *Color*

Black and white: *Blanco y negro* (the opposite way around to how we say it – strange!)

Size: *Tamaño*

Design: *Diseño*

Text: *Texto*

Programme: *Programa*

And most importantly of all…

Price: *Precio*

I arrived to a locked door and spent a few minutes outside, banging frantically on various windows. Eventually an undernourished looking Spaniard approached from the café opposite rattling a bunch of keys. He showed me into his office and workshop. I whipped out my copy of *The Sentinel* magazine under his nose and said I needed a price. He told me what Colin paid for fifteen hundred magazines. As soon as I returned home I skimmed through his last issue to see how much money he made.

"If I double the profit, it will be enough to make a decent living," I said.

"So that means I have to double the price of what Colin charged clients for his adverts."

"Well it's your job," said my Mum. "I'm sure the clients will understand the price rise."

It was time to trawl the streets and make some phone calls to see whether previous advertisers would pay the extra. A few people advised changing the name of the magazine.

"How about calling it *The Sentinella*?" suggested my Mum. Her idea involved a play on words to reflect a female editorship. In Spanish you add 'a' to the end of a word if it is feminine. '*Ella*' also means 'she'. '*Centinela*' in Spanish means a soldier or guard, the same meaning as 'sentinel' in English, so *The Sentinella* is a cross between the two.

The magazine proved harder work than I ever anticipated, but I preferred working like a Trojan than sitting-in and staring at the walls. My Dad and I forgot our recent quarrels and united to become a team. We traipsed around bars and shops to ask if they were interested in advertising. We began by targeting current advertisers and monitoring their reaction to the price increase. The conversation usually went something like this:

My Dad: "Hiya. You've probably heard the news about Colin who used to run *The Sentinel*…?"

Client: "Yes, awful news. How did he die?"

My Dad: "Leukaemia. A sudden death. They caught it too late. My daughter Keidi (a glance in my direction) is continuing with the magazine and today we are visiting all the current advertisers to see if they want to carry on advertising. So do you?"

Client: "Yeah, I don't see why not…"

My Dad: "Well, there's just one thing that has changed, the prices! It seems Colin produced the magazine just as a hobby, but for Keidi this is her job, her future, and so she has to put the prices up in order to make a profit. She has a mortgage to pay you know..." (cringe-worthy moment alert).

At this point most clients switched into the 'we'll have a think about it' mode.

I was really grateful at how much my Dad was helping, but I felt a bit redundant, as I simply stood while he did all the talking. I chose to shut up and listen, simply nodding when appropriate, like some kind of wooden toy.

On recommendation by another client we went to *Bar Billard*, where we met the owner Tom and his lovely wife. It was worth the trip. They took out a quarter page advert and at this crucial stage, every little helped.

The initial feedback seemed promising and every day I added more and more 'definites' to my advertisers list. However, I had major trouble finding a compatible version of the magazine production programme, which I needed. To buy it new cost more than a thousand pounds, but I refused to pay for something that could be acquired for nothing. I endured endless trips to the non-English speaking printer who tried his utmost to find me the right programme, compatible with my laptop. Within three weeks he presented me with four or five versions, but there was a problem with each; whether not compatible with *Windows XP*, Spanish language only, or completely kaput. Realising that the printer's attempts would continue to falter, I tried my luck elsewhere.

Lofty Len, who had recommended the waitress position at Sue and Pete's, sprang to mind. He seemed like the business man type. Len was a very full-on man, who had obviously discovered his entrepreneurial talents a little late in life, but possessed such a strong drive that his determination oozed at the seams. He loved to see someone so young trying to create a business opportunity, and he wanted to help.

"I can't go anywhere with the magazine unless I get hold of this computer programme I need" I said. "Maybe I should just give up."

As soon as he heard the words 'give up' his whole face headed south and he fixed his thinking cap.

"But you can't give up" he stuttered, almost falling off his chair. "You've got this far, you have to see it through. Tell me again what is the name of that computer programme you need? I may know just the man."

He pulled out his 'pay as you go' and called his IT wizard. Thanks to Lofty Len, the following day I finally had the disc in my hands, which I had been after for three weeks or more. I was one step closer to producing the magazine and I was happier than I could remember for an age. This is just one example of how solid the community spirit between ex-pats can be in Spain. As us foreigners are all in the same boat, the atmosphere is generally supportive and encouraging. Len's impeccable help was one of the reasons I made it in Spain, unveiling that good Brits don't mind assisting fellow ex-pats in times of dire need. When problems arise it's reassuring to know there are people who are willing to help and advise, using their knowledge and experience. I liked to think that one day down the line I could offer support and help to someone as Lofty Len had offered me.

Finding employment in Spain is the hardest part of moving here and that's why many Brits go down the self employed road and find a gap in the market to start their own business. The most common new businesses are estate agents, bars, restaurants and shops, but a lot of people also offer services in construction, beauty, gardening and property cleaning and maintenance. In general not all new businesses work and many people have to turn their hand to a number of jobs in order to earn enough to live comfortably here. There are a lot of people, especially those with young families, who struggle to make ends meet.

Now I had the magazine production programme, I needed to work out how to use it! I was under extreme pressure and my row-ometer was hovering on a rather worrying eight. My parents bore the brunt of my argumentative streak, especially my Dad, who I took all my problems out on. I knew this was unfair, especially given how much he was helping me, but the stress I felt was overwhelming. My whole future depended upon the happenings of the next few months.

"Chill Winston" I heard in the back of my head. Desperate to move forward with *The Sentinella*, I swiftly sent off for a guide book describing how to use the computer programme and began e-mailing a technology boffin uncle I hadn't seen for almost a decade. Slowly I began to piece together something which resembled a magazine.

Dealing with the advertising was one of the most important tasks. My Dad and I needed to find another twenty or so companies to make the first issue profitable. Traipsing around foreign lands in summer temperatures exceeding thirty degrees wasn't easy, but little by little, day by day, we managed to find and convince twenty-five new companies to advertise. There were times when I felt like giving up on the spot, when in a whole day we had only managed to sell one advert, but an inner force told me to keep going. We spent one day in Lake Viñuela, an area which is infested with Brits and British businesses. It is located a twenty minute drive away from

Torre del Mar and there are a number of villages surrounding it. In one village we found a firm of English lawyers. The owner was dead fit and I fancied him like mad. He had fair hair, which flopped sexily over his blue eyes and tanned skin.

"Hi I'm Nick" he said. "How can I help you?"

Dad told him about the magazine and the advertising rates. He paid for a business directory listing and said he may want something bigger in the future. Then my Dad did the most embarrassing thing in the world.

"So do you have many friends in the area?" he asked.

"Yeah quite a few" said Nick, looking confused.

"Well maybe Keidi could go out with you some time" he said, looking my way.

"She hasn't been here long and she's looking to meet people."

Nick looked at me with a puzzled expression. I wanted the ground to open and swallow me whole.

"Of course" said Nick. "Here, have my business card. Give me a call whenever you fancy coming out."

"Thanks" I said before fleeing the office.

'Fit Nick' I thought on the way home. I pictured him as my boyfriend and entered his mobile number into my phone, while daydreaming of potential romantic scenarios.

Keidi Keating

Man Magnet

It was July and the weather had really begun to heat up. 'This is it. This is what living in Spain is all about,' I thought, as I rubbed factor ten over my body.

"It's beautiful here" said my Dad on the phone to his brother in the UK

"About thirty-two degrees and clear blue sky. What's it like back there?"

He knew damn well that heavy showers were forecast, but he couldn't help revelling in the fact that we had it better. As a result of the good weather I looked and felt healthier than ever, as if I was blossoming like a flower. Perhaps that was the reason I started attracting men in packs.

The first was the result of an invitation from Pete, a know-all, know-nothing friend of my Mum and Dad's. He invited my parents and I to his villa, en-route to Lake Viñuela. There were breathtaking views from his plot, especially when my eyes landed on his son, Russ, a twenty-five year old who had moved to Spain at the same time as me. He had a toned body and he was good looking in a vague kind of way. One thing's for sure, he certainly hadn't fallen from the ugly tree. As I absorbed the views, lost in a dreamy tunnel, suddenly Russ opened his mouth and I heard him speak for the first time. If I had been a switch, I had just been turned off.

"So 'ave ya lived out 'ere long?' he said in a mumbled northern accent, which made me think of Brookside. It took me a few moments to decipher the sentence.

"Umm, only a few months."

Conversation over. Russ dived in the pool for a dip, presumably because he wanted to show off, or perhaps because he wanted me to strip down to my bikini and follow, but I didn't. I simply sat and watched, as if I was watching a particularly tedious episode of Last of the Summer Wine. He only swam a few lengths, before gracing us once more with his presence.

"D'ya wanna see the views from the roof?" he said, glaring at me with pool water dripping from his torso. His words rolled into each another like a ball knocking down skittles.

"OK"

I followed him up the steep whitewashed steps, which led to the roof top terrace. Russ pointed out distant landmarks and villages.

"... and that white blob to the right of the flat mountain is Benamargosa."

His 'white blob' explanation was just as it appeared, a pond of houses and villas.

"My Dad says five years ago, there were hardly any houses on these mountains" he said. "All you could see back then were the mountains and trees."

"Well I think the white blobs make it look more interesting" I said.

He laughed then his voice turned serious.

"D'ya mind if I have your phone number? We could go out one night. What d'ya reckon?"

I didn't hesitate to reel it off. Despite the Northern accent, Russ was growing on me and at least he was someone to go for a drink with. I left feeling invigorated, with a sense of hope. My inner light was flickering back on. I had turned emotionally empty over the last couple of months, cleared out like a barren desert. I had forgotten how to feel. I had forgotten how to laugh. I had forgotten what it felt like to have a life. Russ offered me hope and the prospect of adventure and discovery.

That evening Russ texted: 'Fancy a drink in Torre this weekend?' How could I possibly turn down the offer of a night on the town? 'Yes, yes, yes!'

I spent an age getting ready, choosing my shortest skirt and a 'pulling' top from the pile of clothes on the floor. Russ wasn't placed in my good books when he turned up late and within the first hour I made the diagnosis that the lights were on, but no one was home. He seemed immature and like most lads his age had an unhealthy obsession with "getting pissed up". Nonetheless, he seemed pretty harmless. When we had exhausted all the subjects safe to talk about on a first date, we hit the nightclubs. We danced and drunk; danced and drunk some more, until we were physically exhausted.

My second date with Russ was at the annual summer fair, in Torre del Mar. In contrast to our first, this was a complete catastrophe, as all he wanted to do was smoke pot. From the moment we met, until the moment we parted, hash was on his brain.

"Mind if I spark up?" he asked, twelve seconds after seeing me for the first time in a week.

"Yeah, no problem" I said. Inside I was fuming, but I retained a cool exterior. I didn't want him knowing I was bothered that pot meant more to him than taking me on the fairground rides. We sat on the beach wall facing the sea. He stuffed a paper full of weed and tobacco, prodding, digging and fumbling with the concoction, until he was satisfied that it was time to roll. Throughout his ritual Russ didn't utter a word. All his energies were sucked into the joint rolling ritual. When he finally lit it, he inhaled as if he was a starving Ethiopian tucking into a three-course meal. I observed the look of relief on his face and thought how sad it was that drugs have this effect on people. Russ clearly 'needed' his fix of weed. After a few inhalations Russ offered the half disappeared joint to me, waving it under my nose.

"No. Not for me." I said. "I don't do drugs."

"Your loss" he said, before assassinating the remainder. He flicked the butt on to the sand and seemed content simply sitting, his eyes glazed and bloodshot, his brain on a different planet. At the fair the sounds skipping from rides, music systems, huge speakers and happy crowds were deafening. Lights and colours danced in front of my eyes and the smells of fresh candy floss and hot dogs wafted into my nostrils. Disappointingly, Russ wasn't keen on venturing on any of the rides with me.

"Oh go on" I said, eyeing a really cool upside down roller coaster, which projected the screaming passengers every way imaginable.

"This one will be a right laugh."

He shook his head. "Nah…" he said. "Not for me. I don't mind having a go on the dodgems though."

With that he raced on to a stationary and unoccupied car, shouting back at me to find a free vehicle. I didn't have time to think otherwise so leapt into a yellow and green one, almost knocking over a mother and daughter team. When I thought about spending the night at the fair this is not what I had in mind. Racing around a platform, with a sea of testosterone seeping teenagers, wasn't my idea of a good night. I gripped the steering wheel tighter, as Russ rammed into me from behind. My head almost sprang off my neck and I banged my elbow on the car door. This boy sure knew how *not* to treat his date. He wasn't going out of his way to impress me. Ten minutes and four bruises later the dodgems stopped.

"That was wicked" Russ said. "Let's go again."

"Uhmm, not for me" I said. "I'll watch."

"Boring!" Russ shouted as he ran to a vacant car for another turn.

I stood on the sidelines and watched the cars whiz past. Russ repeated the dodgems four times on the trot and he had the audacity to call me boring. What kind of guy takes his date to a funfair and selfishly only goes on the rides he wants? I hated him.

"What's up with yer?" He asked when I had stayed silent for around eight minutes.

"Absolutely nothing" I said. "You're just being paranoid. Must be all that pot you smoke."

I liked my answer. I felt like I had got one over on him, especially as the underhand comment shut him up. I was glad. Every word that escaped his mouth infuriated me, plus his Brookside accent was really getting my goat.

"We may as well call it a night, eh?" said Russ after a further ten minutes of silence.

"Yes let's" I agreed. He walked me home, while chain-smoking joints.

"Thanks for taking me to the fair" I said. "I had a brilliant time." I said this with just the slightest hint of sarcasm. I hoped it might make Russ think what a total arse-wipe he had been.

"That's all right" he said, smiling. "I'm really glad you enjoyed it. We'll have to meet again soon, yeah?"

"Of course" I uttered, through gritted teeth.

My friend Nicole arrived a few days later for a holiday. It was the first time I had seen her for four and a half months and I was as happy as a lark. Nicole was one of my best friends in the UK. I got to know her via another friend when I was eighteen. She has long dark blonde hair and beautiful wide eyes, surrounded by the longest eyelashes I have ever seen. Since seeing the film she has always reminded me of Bridget Jones, mainly because despite being gorgeous and lovely, she never has much luck with men. When she turned up I felt like I had seen her only yesterday. We picked up from where we had left off, when she dropped me at Gatwick Airport that cold March morning, so I could catch my one way flight to Málaga. I needed to make up for four and a half months of diabolical social life, in ten days. For the first few hours we simply plotted in a bar with drinks while she reeled off all the gossip about our circle of friends.

"Jenny's split up with Dan because she met another guy…Si and Dave are sleeping together…Katie thinks she might be pregnant but is scared to do a test…Amy walked in on Sean with another girl and flipped her lid…"

Her tales made me realise nothing had changed. I was glad I had chosen to chuck in the towel and move to Spain, the UK sounded like the same monotonous story. During Nicole's stay I restocked on social encounters and boosted my previously flagging confidence ten-fold. In all honesty I was a bit of a man magnet during her visit. My 'single and available' aura must have been glowing brightly.

One of the men I met was called Jose, who homed in on me during a night out in Torrox Costa. Nicole and I were dancing with our 'we don't care what the hell we look like' hats on.

"Hola" said Jose. "You are very beautiful."

"Gracias" I answered, blushing. He continued to ask where I lived, why I had moved from England, how old I was and all the other questions that two newly-meets ask. My Spanish was appalling and his English was worse, but we scraped through the night. As I was drunk Jose didn't seem too bad. He had all the typical Spanish attributes and a friendly enough face. He wasn't too short or too fat and he certainly wasn't ugly. Nicole was stuck with Jose's geeky friend, who was tall and wiry, like one of those bendy animals you can manipulate into new shapes. In the early hours Jose dropped us at my apartment, where we were staying that night. He asked if we could meet outside at eleven the following morning.

"Yeahhhh sssurrre" I replied, slurring my words like an alcoholic. Morning arrived and Nicole and I crawled out of bed with heavy heads.

"I've got a hangover" moaned Nicole.

"Me too" I said "My head feels like it's made of quick dry concrete."

"You only have five minutes before you're meeting Jose"

"Shit!" I had completely forgotten "Ummm, I think I'm going to pass. I was very drunk. I didn't mean it and also I look a mess."

Our conversation was interrupted by loud hoots coming from outside.

"Oh my God, that's probably him" Nicole said, laughing. She peeked around the edge of the window and leapt back giggling.

"Told you so. He's outside, walking up and down the street looking in all the balconies."

Nicole and I hid, glancing out the window every now and then to see whether Jose was still there. Half an hour later an angry sounding car sped off.

That evening we went for a Chinese meal in Torre. A bunch of hardened looking geezers sat in *Bar Billard* opposite. One of them, a large lad with a beer-belly, plonked his bum at our table.

"Mind if I join you?"

"By all means" I answered. It was too late anyway, as he already had. His name was Gavin and he was a big man with a big personality. His confidence oozed at the seams. At one point I thought he might pop.

"So what brings you two lovely ladies to a shit hole like this?" he asked with a contagious grin on his chubby but handsome face.

I told him my parents lived here and that soon I would be moving into my own place in El Morche.

"Lovely" he said. "I live just up the road from there, in Algarrobo Costa. I've got a four-bedroom penthouse with a pool on the roof. Perfect it is. I love it. It's really spacious and the roof is like a sun-trap, no kidding. There's an underground garage, under floor heating, air conditioning and everything. You'll have to come and have a look sometime. The neighbours are all Spanish but it could be worse, they could be English!" He laughed.

Wow, this man knew how to talk (mostly about himself). He clearly didn't know how to shut up. Gavin continued ranting about his "fabulous apartment" which really sounded the same as every other apartment on the Costa del Sol. Nicole nodded like a jack in the box, with a glazed face. I couldn't take any more of his apartment. I needed to change the subject.

"How old are you?" I asked. He was off again.

"Twenty-seven"

Nicole opened her mouth to speak, but Gavin cut in.

"Before you say anything, I know I look older than that, but really, I'm twenty-seven. How about you two lovely ladies?"

Wow! He actually asked us a question. He self-steered the talk away from himself. Maybe this guy wasn't so predictable after all. We had him playing the guessing game before we finally revealed our ages.

"I would have thought you were older than that" he said, staring at me. "Not that you look it, but Tom in *Bar Billard* over there told me he's advertising in the first issue of your magazine. I just thought a magazine Editor would be a lot older than twenty-three."

"There's a lot I've done for a twenty-three year old" I said with sexy undertones. 'Oh my God. What was I doing? Was I flirting with this guy?' He erupted into laughter.

"Let me buy you girls a drink" he offered. "What will it be?"

While he was gone, Nicole and I discussed him.

"He fancies you so badly" she said. "I can tell. He can't stop staring at you."

"No he doesn't" I said. Although I knew he did and it felt good. Despite the fact that he looked older than twenty-seven and was overweight, I was glad he found me attractive. I needed the compliments in order to re-instate my confidence levels to their old healthy heights. As the night progressed we told Gavin how we were planning on visiting Marbella the next day.

"Really? How are you getting there?" he said.

"Well, I don't have my car over here yet, so we'll have to take the bus."

"Sod that. You don't want to be sitting around waiting for buses all day. I'm going to Marbella tomorrow to see my lawyer. I have four new businesses to sort out. You may as well jump in with me." I guessed that was an invitation.

"OK. What time shall we meet?" We sorted out the whens and wheres, then told Gavin we had to go.

"Just one thing," he said. "I'd better tell you. My car is a right old rust bucket, a Ford Fiesta, the old model."

We couldn't believe it. The man who had a lawyer in Marbella, four businesses on the go and a penthouse apartment with air conditioning and under floor heating, drove a rusty Ford Fiesta. Something didn't add up and our faces must have spoke volumes.

"You don't want to be walking home alone at this time of night," he said. "I'll give you a lift back now if you want? Then you can see what I mean."

He led us to a road of parked cars. My eyes scanned them for an 'old Ford Fiesta' but I couldn't see anything of the kind. The car next to us made a popping noise as the electric locks unlatched. I nearly fainted when I saw it. He had the latest Mercedes, the kind of car we all dream about and will never afford. Gavin laughed like a disturbed donkey.

"Got you both!" he joked.

This man's fun personality was growing on me. He didn't take life seriously and that was an attractive attribute. Gavin drove us the one-minute ride to my parent's apartment block. We felt rather like chauffeur-driven royalty as we left the sparkling silver Merc.

"See you tomorrow" we called as Gavin sped off.

The following morning, we hitched our lift in the head turning mobile and as predicted Gavin talked non-stop. Marbella is some seventy kilometres away from Torre del Mar, west of Málaga, and it is possible to access it either via the motorway or the coast road. For speed and economy reasons, the motorway is always the best option. To arrive by bus would have involved one to Málaga Bus Station and a second direct to Marbella.

Nicole and I started our mission at a wee delicatessen recommended by Gavin. There were piles of cream filled cakes to turn our tummies, alongside small but intricately adorned biscuits, fancy chocolates and wrapped gifts. The shop depicted wealth and glamour, both of which we had expected from Marbella, so it was the ideal starting point.

"Bang goes my diet, again" said Nicole as we filled our tummies with chocolate and cream involved morsels.

Afterwards, we looked around some designer shops, then hit the beach for a standard holiday photography session. The beach in the main area of Marbella isn't huge, but there are rocky paths leading out to sea which are fun to walk along. After exhausting Marbella we walked along the coast to Puerto Banus.

"I can't wait to reach the harbour and see all the yachts" said Nicole.

"Maybe we might meet a nice yachtsman to take us to sea" I said.

"Oooh that would be so excellent."

Puerto Banus is a quaint port, retaining much of its traditional character and style, yet attracting modern, wealthy businessmen and women. Men sat in coffee shops tapping away at their laptops. Ladies wore high heels, designer suits and shades, walking pictures of success and wealth. It was a real eye opener to see the yachts, all lined up waiting to be taken to sea and set free. Their sails flapped excitedly, singing with the wind. Some donned Union Jacks flying high, others contained young crowds sipping cocktails and living the good life. As Nicole and I strutted along, we pouted at any young attractive yachtsmen who caught our eye, hoping they might invite us on as their guests. Sadly, our pulling techniques went unnoticed.

"You never know Gavin might know someone with a yacht" said Nicole with a glint in her eye. She nudged me a few times as she spoke. "Maybe he even has one himself. He's got everything else."

I didn't say anything. At the back of my mind (hiding in my subconscious) I knew I would see Gavin again, but I didn't want to admit it right then.

"Let's stop for a drink, I'm so thirsty." I said, swiftly changing the subject.

The busy café overlooked the port, so it was an ideal spot to man and yacht spy. I was pleasantly surprised when a handsome waiter, who had served our drinks, asked for my telephone number. He wanted to meet me for a coffee one day. He didn't speak a word of English but I understood him. It made me feel important and clever, as if I was finally getting somewhere with the language. The barrier was still there of course, but there were now small holes visible, as if a woodpecker had been at it. The waiter's name was Simo, aged twenty-six. He was tall, normal build and had a handsome clean-cut face and kind eyes with the customary dark hair. He looked happy, content and comfortable in his skin.

"Oh, you're so lucky" said Nicole. "That's really romantic, the way he came up to you like that. How do you do it?"

That was just it, I had no idea. Suddenly, miraculously, I was attracting men in their droves and I had no idea why or how. As my man magnet was positive, I also received a random text message from Nick, the fit accountant in Lake Viñuela, asking if I wanted to meet for a drink in Torre del Mar some time. I couldn't believe my luck. I had bored Nicole to tears describing him, now she was going to meet him in the flesh. With Nicole there it felt less like a date and more like friends meeting. Even so, I was a bundle of nerves when he turned up. He sent electricity pulsating throughout my entire body. He looked dead fit with bleach blond streaks accentuating his messy hair. Nicole fancied him rotten too.

"You're so lucky if you manage to nab him" she said when he had left.

Nicole also met Russ one evening, who joined us in Torre to "get pissed up." He was another one who was chasing me. There was Jose, Gavin, Nick, Simo and Russ. I was literally fighting them off!

"Sorry for the night of the fair" said Russ, when we were alone. "Why don't we 'give it a go' and see how we get on, you know…"

I thought for a few seconds, with a brain half drowned in vodka and coke.

"Yeah, OK." The words tumbled out before I could stop them. Deep down I knew it was hardly worth the effort starting anything with Russ, as he wasn't exactly boyfriend material.

Amidst all the men I also met a new girlfriend during Nicole's stay. We were sitting outside a beach-front café when a woman wearing khaki combats, red T-shirt and trainers approached our table. She had very short light brown hair and pretty sky blue eyes.

"Hi there, are you two English by any chance?" she asked with a zesty voice.

"We sure are" said Nicole.

"Excellent" said the mystery female. "I run creative writing groups in the area. Can I join you for a minute to tell you some more?"

Her 'free spirit' aura shone brightly like a light bulb.

"I'm a writer too" I said. "Of course, sit down."

It was one thing to meet a new potential friend, but a writer friend was something I had never had before. Most of my pals didn't actually share my interests, they were all just people I got on with. Having a writer friend would be insightful and interesting. We could share tips, inspire and encourage each other to continue practising our talent.

"My name's Anna by the way" said the casually dressed woman, as she collapsed into a chair and summoned the attention of the waiter with a raise of her hand and a warm smile. "I live in Cómpeta."

Cómpeta is one of the mountain villages of the Axarquia region, situated some thirty minutes inland. In recent years it has grown unbelievably, becoming an increasingly popular home for ex-pats, especially the creative sorts.

"I'm Keidi" I said. "And this is Nicole, who's visiting from the UK."

"Nice to meet you both" she said. "Thought I'd just pop over to tell you about my weekly writing groups I run here in Torre, for people who want to have books published, or learn how to become better writers." She handed us a leaflet.

"I'm also a 'book doctor" she said chuckling.

"A book doctor?"

"Yeah, I help to make people's manuscripts better for sending off to agents and publishers."

Anna's life and background sounded interesting, she thought mine did too, and we had a lot to talk about. Not only that but she seemed fun and intelligent.

"How about running a writing competition in the first issue of *The Sentinella*?" she suggested. "I could judge it if you like?"

"That's a good idea" I said.

We exchanged phone numbers. I knew we would keep in touch. I liked the fact she had such an open-minded, spiritual outlook on life. She acted rather like a catalyst to my own thoughts and feelings, even if I hadn't applied many of them by that stage.

Where's It Bin?

Why is it that whenever you have a good stint in life, the aftermath is a web of downright misery? When Nicole left Spain I felt seriously lonely again. I couldn't stomach the thought of no more nights out, so met Russ. We planned to stay in my apartment after a night in Nerja. After all, we were apparently 'giving it a go,' whatever 'it' meant. We sunbathed on the beach during the day, sharing my towel, as his looked like it belonged to a mouse.

"What on earth do you propose to do with that thing?" I asked, eyeing the minute rag he pulled from his bag. "It looks more like a flannel."

He didn't appreciate my humour, appearing to take the flannel comment to heart. Not a great deal of banter exchanged between us. I tried conversing a few times, but Russ was more interested in snoozing. Fortunately, small talk wasn't strictly necessary. The beach was so relaxing that my mind drifted into a world of pleasant daydreams. Warm sun pounded upon my skin, the sweet sounds of children playing echoed in my ears, coupled with the sea's song. Occasionally I smelt the smouldering of fresh sardines.

"Oh yes, this is the life…" and then I looked across at Russ "…Well almost".

Later, we arrived at a bustling Nerja. As the night progressed I realised the level of Russ' immaturity. His true colours emerged and I didn't like them. In one bar he took an obvious disliking to the male bartender for no apparent reason. At the same time he took an even more obvious liking to the female bartender.

"Three shots each of the strongest you have" he said, slamming a fifty down, as if he had plenty more where that came from. He necked the trio of green concoctions simultaneously, egging me to do the same.

"How fast can you run?" he asked the male bartender out of nowhere. The barman looked shocked at the haphazard question and a little intrigued.

"Fast enough. Why?"

"I'll bet I'm faster" Russ said. "Let's have a race."

The bartender shook his head.

"Nah. You're having a laugh aren't you mate."

"Come on" pleaded Russ, like an ego-hungry schoolboy. "Let's race. I want to thrash you."

Mr Bartender was clearly becoming vexed by Russ's hopes of glory. I could see he wanted to knock him down a peg or two. The race banter continued for a while, each comment more arrogant than the last, until eventually Russ wore him down.

"OK, let's race."

"Cool! To the end of the square, touch the wall then back," cut in Russ, like a newly sharpened knife.

"You watching girls?" He ran his eyes over the pretty barmaid and I. "You're looking at a winner here."

I wanted an alien space-craft to hover overhead and beam me up. I hoped everyone in the vicinity of Russ and his big head would realise he was *not* my boyfriend. I felt embarrassed by his rash egotistic behaviour and all just because he fancied the barmaid. I could see why, mind. She was thin and gorgeous with huge eyes and long brown hair hanging around her shoulders in neat pigtails. If I were a man I probably would have fancied her too, but I also knew she thought he was a total waste of space. Every time Russ looked away she rolled her eyes to the heavens, as if to say, "pleeeeease."

Russ and the barman re-entered the bar panting and Russ had his arms held high with a victorious look spread across his face.

"You won then?" I said with a hint of sarcasm.

"Of course" he said, so as many people as possible could hear. "I am the champion…"

"Come on" I said. "I've had enough of this bar, let's move on."

"What's up with yer?" Russ called after me. "What did I do?"

I didn't fancy drinking on my own, so hung about outside, hidden around a corner. I knew he would follow me out. Everyone in that bar detested him and even with a head the size of his, he would soon acknowledge the fact. It took just thirty seconds. He bounded up to me swigging from a *Bud* bottle.

"Why did you leave?" Russ asked. "I like it in there."

"Well I don't" I said. "You embarrassed me. You were acting like an imbecile."

"Good to know you think so much of me" he said. "Come on tell me what's really up? Do you love me? Is that what it is?"

I couldn't believe this boy. I almost choked on my own saliva.

"Love you? Definitely not, I'm still trying to work out if I even like you."

With that quick-witted remark Russ looked offended. I was glad. He needed something to deflate his head and I liked the fact that it was my words. I imagined sticking a pin in a balloon until it went pop.

"What d'ya wanna do now then?" he asked after an awkward pause.

"Well I don't know about you, but I'm going home" I said, heading in the direction of the taxi rank.

"What? It's only two o'clock. You can't go home now."

"Watch me!"

I couldn't possibly stay out any longer with this rat. It didn't cross my mind that he would clamber in the taxi with me. He would want to stay out drinking and acting like a prat, surely? No.

"I assume it's still OK to stay over?" he asked.

"I guess so" I said. I was exhausted and could barely speak. It was easier just to agree.

At mine, Russ undressed and leapt into my bed. I hated the thought of his skin on my bed sheets. I climbed into the other side of bed fully dressed and shuffled as close to the edge as possible without falling out. I turned so my back faced Russ. That way he would know not to try anything on. The message didn't register. I felt his hands running over my fully clothed body, and I freaked out and dashed up to sit on the balcony.

"You've got a serious problem" Russ called after me.

It was a mild peaceful night so I enjoyed sitting on the balcony alone, admiring the glittering stars. It was far better than lying next to Russ. Occasionally my silence was interrupted by an accelerating motorbike or the drones of Russ' pig-like snores. I thought about the last few weeks and all that had happened. I smiled. I had really enjoyed all the male attention. I felt young again. My adventure in Spain had really kicked off and this was only the beginning.

After Nicole's visit and meeting such an array of men, I realised that my initial observation of 'there are only oldies living in Spain' was wrong. I just hadn't been looking in the right places. That night in Nerja I had seen piles of young English people.

I spared a thought for Simo, the Spanish waiter I had met in Puerto Banus, who had asked for my number. He had texted a few times asking me for a drink but I declined all his offers. Now there was a decent man, just my luck that he lived on the other side of the costa.

The following day I erased Russ' number from my mobile. There was no way I was communicating with that boy again. Ever.

Next weekend arrived and I couldn't face staying in, so in a state of desperation I texted Gavin, who responded immediately. It was the feria (fair) weekend in El Morche and he collected me in his fancy Merc'. He had made an effort to dress up and looked pleasing to the eye in his pale cotton trousers and white shirt. In all honesty, I dressed up too. I wore a short skirt, low cut vest top and shoes with heels. I felt sexy and confident. I applied red lipstick and sprayed perfume on my neck and wrists. The atmosphere at the feria was loud and heavy. There was music blasting, rides whooshing, teens shouting, children playing and adults chatting. I felt one hundred per cent alive and above all, I felt happy. Gavin made me feel safe. I didn't need to worry about him darting on to the dodgems, leaving me standing there like a lemon. I didn't need to fret about him chatting up other girls, or challenging random people to running races. I could simply relax, enjoy his company and above all, have a good time. We ordered *tinto de verano* (red wine with lemonade) and ate *pinchitos* (meat on sticks). The conversation was flowing as fast as the drinks and we were channelled into the same frequency and wavelength. I learned that he strived for success just like me, and I loved his determined nature. He asked me a lot of questions about *The Sentinella* magazine.

"So you make the money from the adverts then? How much profit do you think you will make on the first issue? Have you edited magazines before?"

I wondered why he was so interested, but I was happy to let some of the built up information off my chest. As we chatted, I noticed what nice eyes Gavin had. I pictured myself as Little Red Riding Hood in front of the big bad wolf.

"My, what big eyes you have" I would say donning a red cloak and holding a straw basket. I chose to forget about the mouth. That was big too.

After a few too many *tintos de verano* my bladder was ready to explode.

"I think there are some of those port-a-loo thingies on the beach" said Gavin.

Then I remembered that we were in El Morche and in just three minutes we could step inside my apartment, where a clean barely-used loo was waiting. I told Gavin my plan.

"Great! You can give me a tour while we're there," he said. I laughed.

"A tour?! That will take approximately thirty seconds."

En-route Gavin pulled me close, and gave me a huge and unexpected snog. I was lost for words, but he made me feel at ease again.

"Sorry for that" he said. "I couldn't help myself. I've wanted to do that all night."

I left feeling confused about my feelings towards Gavin.

Back to the daily grind. Torre del Mar was now heaving with tourists and holiday hungry Spanish, most of whom took the whole of August off work. Many businesses shut down completely at this time of the year. During the day the Spanish holiday makers sprawled themselves on the beach, complete with deckchairs, umbrellas, canopies, cool boxes, hampers, tables and toys for the children. They went to great lengths to ensure they had all they would possibly need and more just in case. It seemed to be the fashion to buy bags of *pipas* (seeds) and sit breaking them with their teeth and flinging the empty shells on to the sand.

Come night time the Spanish congested the *heladerias* (ice-cream parlours) until the wee hours. To see so many people having fun was invigorating and encouraging, but parking in the town became a nightmare. Many of the tourists who had travelled down from Jaén or Madrid simply parked their cars in the same spot for the entire duration of their stay, often eight weeks or more. This made free places limited and often my Dad would navigate the town a few times before finding a space to leave his car.

In the meantime *The Sentinella's* first issue deadline was growing ever closer. I was a little worried about the appearance of some of the adverts. The colour pages looked a little ropey, but there wasn't enough time to seek further help. I would just have to make do and hope the advertisers would be happy. Most of them had warmed to me anyway. They loved to see a young girl making a go of a business in Spain.

I received a text from Sarah, the nanny who I had been introduced to a couple of months back. She said she was now living here, high up in the mountains, and invited me out with some locals for a night in Torre del Mar. It was great to see her again. I knew she would make a fabulous friend, whom I could trust and rely on. Her older brother Rob, who was twenty-seven, also joined us.

He struck me as the deep and meaningful type, with slightly odd tendencies I couldn't put my finger on.

My first issue of *The Sentinella* was coming along nicely. There were 36 pages to fill with text and adverts. My Dad spent one morning wandering around Torre del Mar armed with his camera to take a front cover shot.

"What kind of thing are you after?" he asked.

"Anything" I said. "Just use your imagination, I have no idea."

My brief was useless, but he returned with a whole load of shots to choose from. There were statues, palm trees, beach shots, orange trees and many more.

"What are these four at the end here, Dad? They appear to be of some kind of bin?"

"Oh…I was just messing about. Just saw the bin there and thought I'd take some photos of it." A thought darted into my mind.

"That's it. That's the shot I'm going to use for the front cover…the bin."

My Dad looked at me in bewilderment. All that time he had spent agonising over the best shots and I used the very last photos he had only taken as a joke; the bin! I already had the by-line in my head. 'Where's It Bin?' Colin had passed away eight weeks ago and I knew people were talking about *The Sentinel* and why they hadn't seen any copies around. Many still didn't know the dreadful news of his death. The front page photo and headline would intrigue people enough to pick it up. I thought the new title would aid too. *The Sentinel* was now *The Sentinella*, a word which nobody would understand the meaning of. I didn't fully understand it myself. I also thought of a catchy phrase to include on the front page of the first and future issues. I thought about the product, a small magazine. It was small enough to fit into people's bags; a magazine which would travel around with people and not be left sitting at home on the coffee table. Then it came to me: 'The little mag that fits in your bag.' Bingo! My mind was behaving rather like a shiny jewel. I wanted to put it on display so people would admire it. I had forgotten just how creative I could be when I tried.

My favourite part of the magazine production process was writing the Editor's column. I had always dreamed of writing my own slot in a newspaper or magazine. At the age of eighteen I landed a full-time job as trainee reporter on a local newspaper. I saw myself working my way up to Editor and penning the opening spill every week. How I would love that. Now it was happening. My dream was materialising.

The Sentinella, September 2004

"I hope you enjoy reading the first issue as much as I enjoyed producing it. I would, of course, appreciate your feedback. What would you like to see more of/ less of / never see again…? There will also be a letters page so if you want to get something off your chest, write to me at the address on page three and it may or may not get printed!"

Keidi Keating, Editor

My name at the end shone and I reflected on what a lucky young lady I was, to be in this position. As I read my column I spared a thought for Colin and his parents. My lucky break was another man's ending. I owed him such a lot and all I could offer was recognition and remembrance. This thought compelled me to include a tribute to Colin on the first available page, plus an eternal dedication to him in each issue. I didn't want to steal his business. He was the one who originally founded the magazine, so his name should live on.

Aside from the editorial content, which as a writer I found relatively easy, the design work also had to be taken into consideration. Firstly I needed to design a logo for *The Sentinella*. I typed the two words then spent the next few hours trying every font available. When I had decided upon my favourite, I placed it in a yellow box. Mission accomplished.

Selling was not something I had ever done, or indeed ever imagined doing in my life. Luckily my Dad knew the principles.

"Why don't you go in this shop yourself and I'll wait outside?"

"No way" I said. "I don't know what to say. What if they say no? I'll feel like a right Muppet."

"OK, watch and learn" he joked.

I knew I could do it, but I also knew that all the time my Dad came round with me, he would do it and that was the easy option. But one morning as I passed Lofty Len's bar, I popped in to say hello.

"Hi there gal" he said. "To what do I owe such a fine visitor?"

"I was just passing. Thought I'd call in and see how you are?"

"All good here. Made a killing last night. We were packed solid."

My head ticked. 'He had a good night…that means he made a lot of money, so he will want to spend some on advertising.'

"If you want some more busy nights you ought to advertise in the first issue of *The Sentinella*" I said with a half flirtatious, half sweet smile. Lofty Len chuckled. He clearly knew my game.

"Ah, I see" he followed. "That's the real reason you came in, innit? Touting for business, eh?"

"It's just that I'm having trouble selling the back page" I said in a moment of weakness "I thought you might like to have it, at a discount of course?"

"How much we talking?" asked Len.

A price fell from the top of my head and he agreed. 'Cool,' I thought. 'Selling advertising is easier than I thought.'

My advertisers list was growing larger by the day, but there still weren't enough. I spent a day flicking through the rival magazines, listing companies to call and persuade to advertise. Opposed to cold calling on foot, via the telephone I felt a lot more confident. All my jobs in the UK had involved regular telephone contact with clients, so I was used to communicating in this way.

As we sought new advertisers I noticed how friendly most of the business owners were. On the other hand there were the few abrupt, pigheaded ones, who interrupted with a sharp "no" before we even had the chance to announce what we were offering. In total my father and I sold thirty-six adverts for the first issue, plus the business directory listings at the back. The word about *The Sentinella* was spreading and I was poised for a successful launch.

The Launch

The printer in Torre del Mar promised he would return from holiday in time to have the first issue of *The Sentinella* ready for distribution on September the first. As the last week of August approached I traipsed to the office every morning and evening. Each time my eyes met shuttered windows and a bolted door and I was growing increasingly worried. I had promised all my advertisers that the first issue would be distributed on the first day of September . If I didn't meet the deadline I would be a laughing stock. Finally, on the very last day of August he answered my telephone call, so I ran to his office immediately. My heart sank when he told me the magazine would take ten days to print. I felt like giving up, but something inside told me to persevere.

"Maybe we should drive around some other printing companies" said my Dad. "We might even find a cheaper one."

"Yeah, OK" I said, utterly deflated. "We may as well."

Three attempts later we found one on the other side of Torre del Mar, who was expensive but quick. He was charging an extra three hundred Euros for the luxury of staples in the magazines. I snorted at the sum. Almost a quarter of the total cost again, just to make the magazines into magazines. I couldn't believe his audacity. I was desperate, but not that desperate, so asked him just to print the pages. When they were ready in a few days, we would have to staple fifteen hundred copies of the magazine together ourselves.

"I'll help if you like" said Gavin on the phone that afternoon. I had started seeing Gavin three or four times a week. He had even shown me his luxury penthouse with the roof top pool, which I had heard so much about on that first night. It was nice, but not amazing as I had expected, and it wasn't a penthouse, just fourth floor. Gavin sure liked to exaggerate, but I accepted that as part of his ample character.

When I saw his apartment my first thought was 'mess,' as there was a lot of it. Empty coke cans littered the floor and tables and crumb filled take-away boxes covered the sofa. Piles of papers and business documents were strewn everywhere imaginable, with no filing system. Amidst the lot sat a laptop computer and a few mobile phones.

All this while, I drummed-in to Gavin that we were 'just friends'. I liked him, but I was unwilling to become romantically involved. He set me free from my parents' apartment, where I felt like I had outstayed my welcome.

As the magazine deadline approached, I became ever more argumentative and my moods were up and down like a yo-yo. One day I would feel so positive and could see myself running a popular magazine and making a decent living, while other days I would wonder why I was bothering, believing the magazine would fail and that it would never make enough profit for me to live a good life. I wanted to be rich. I hated the thought of struggling financially for the rest of my life. I had endured constant penny-counting throughout my time in the UK. Paying a mortgage at the age of nineteen wasn't easy. I just about earned enough every month to pay all the bills and have a pittance left to spend. I had to budget strictly, frequently turning down social invitations in order to pay the mortgage. I envisaged myself waving goodbye to all that and welcoming wealth with open arms. I wanted to be rich and successful and I knew running *The Sentinella* was a good start. I had been offered an opportunity on a plate and I had to taste the contents. At the time I had no idea what a big meal I would make of it!

Gavin called at least twice a day for random conversations, mostly about silly things, which always brought a smile to my face. One day he asked if I fancied a night out with a twist.

"How do you fancy seeing Van Morrison in concert tonight, in *Marbella*?" He emphasised the word *'Marbella'* slowly.

"You mean *the* Van Morrison?" I said. "The real one?"

He laughed. "Of course the real one, you 'nana. I've got free tickets, and invitations to the after party at *Silks* on the beach."

"Cool" I said, with an obvious lack of enthusiasm in my voice.

"You do know what *Silks* on the beach is?"

"Uhm, well actually, no" I said, embarrassed about my lack of knowledge.

"It's the place where all the celebs hang out. They all go there. It's the place to be. So what do you reckon? Are you up for it? I can pick you up at seven."

Thoughts raced through my mind. 'What would I wear? Did I have enough time to get ready? Who else was going?' Yes, that's what I really wanted to know.

"There are three other couples and my best mate John. They're really good mates of mine. You'll like them all, I promise."

'Three other couples' The words bounded across my brain, ringing in my ears. Gavin and I weren't a couple, I thought he understood that.

"Look, Gav, I'd love to come, but only if you accept that we'll only be going as friends?"

"Sure thing. If that's what's worrying you, forget it. I won't try anything on, I promise. I'll be as good as gold."

"In that case, you're on. See you at seven."

I pulled on a stunning black dress, attached some simple silver jewellery and made-up to fit in with millionaire sorts.

Gavin's friends were a varying bunch, they were all stinking rich and drugged up to their eyeballs. I didn't like them much, one in particular, who appeared to be the leader of the pack and reminded me of Austin Powers. All he spoke about was money, his yacht, money, his sports car, money, cocaine, money, the bird he was shagging behind his missus' back, and money. Despite the ill company I wasn't prepared to let them ruin my night.

The show was amazing and Van was on top form. Halfway through the night the champagne reacted with my head, and if Gavin and I were 'just friends', we certainly weren't normal ones. Post-concert we joined the beach party at *Silks*, where I saw some really eye-opening sights. Old men smoked cigars with busty woman draped over their scrawny bodies. Topless girls giggled in an eight person jacuzzi, joined by male hunks with large biceps. Half-naked couples lay on partially hidden hammocks, whispering sweet nothings into each other's ears. A live band injected heart and soul to liven up the area with soft rock. Gavin and I held hands gently and he stroked my hand with his index finger, looking smitten as he stared into my eyes. The party atmosphere cleared my mind completely, I felt so alive and I didn't want the night to end, but all good things have to, it's one of the rules of life. In the early hours, we headed back to Torre del Mar and Gavin's fun loving personality transformed into serious mode.

"So what does tonight mean?" he said. "Just friends? Yeah right!"

I laughed. "Well I suppose we could see how things go."

"Really?" Gavin asked. "So I can tell people you're my *girlfriend* then?"

When I said "see how things go" I hadn't meant to launch into a full blown relationship. Gavin had a great knack of hearing information selectively; but he seemed so excited at the prospect of me as his girlfriend, that I couldn't possibly throw a spanner in the works.

"OK" I said. "You can!"

A few days before the first magazine was due to launch, we still hadn't received it. It was a stressful lead-up. When the loose magazine pages (without staples) were finally ready I was astonished at the quantity. There were piles of them, all fastened in separate stacks. The smell of freshly printed pages was wonderful, like some kind of drug. I inhaled the poignant aroma with content.

As I glared at the mass of pages, I knew the stapling operation would be huge.

I couldn't wait to see the 'Where's It Bin?' front cover, but back at home it was nowhere to be seen. I double and treble checked, then my stomach went all jittery.

"Oh my God, they haven't given us the front page" I said. "We can't launch a magazine without a front page. What are we going to do? Dad..? This stupid magazine. I've had enough of it already."

"Calm down" said my Dad. "We'll go back to the printer and find out. He's probably just forgotten to give us a pile. Don't worry."

Easy for him to say, but I was worried. I didn't know how to take Spanish business people at that time. I had heard so many cases of un-professionalism.

My heart was racing as we pulled up outside, but the printer had already found the extra pile. It felt like a force from above was trying to prevent us from bringing out *The Sentinella*. I wondered if Colin was angry. I thought about all the problems we had encountered to reach this stage. First we couldn't access Colin's computer, then we had to find a compatible version of the magazine production programme. I had nightmares working out how to use it. The printer was closed at the time he was meant to be printing the first issue so we had to find a new one. The new one was charging too much for stapling. The front page was missing and then there was the mammoth stapling operation. The whole process certainly didn't run like clockwork!

Gavin was almost as excited as me about the first issue.

"We'll have that stapling done in no time," he said. He changed his tune when he saw the pages piled high in my Dad's boot.

"My God. This is going to take ages,"

"I'll make the piles and you do the stapling," I said. The stapler was larger than normal and a little stiff and Gavin had bigger hands than me. I worked like Superwoman, with no break from three in the afternoon until six o'clock the following morning. I slept for a few hours in the spare room, before rising to yet more stacking.

Delivering the magazines was an enjoyable task. Delivery involved loading up the car and stopping outside all the English-owned businesses to leave a pile in their premises. We drove right along the coast, from Rincon de la Victoria to Nerja, spanning some twenty-five kilometres, then up the mountains to Cómpeta, Lake Viñuela, Benamargosa and Riogordo. In fact we covered most of the Axarquia region. By the end of it we were totally exhausted. I collapsed on to the nearest chair and stayed there until I had enough energy to haul myself to bed.

Although five days later than promised, none of the clients seemed particularly fazed. Instead they greeted the new publication with open arms.

"We've had so many people coming in asking for this" said one client, as he held it up approvingly.

"It looks fantastic" said another, as if admiring a Picasso painting.

I didn't think so. Being self-stapled, most of the pages were wonky and the adverts in the middle looked diabolical. None of the colours were bright enough and my design skills drastically needed improving.

It was a buzz collecting the advertising payments, but I felt a sense of guilt when taking it from certain clients. Not many instigated the payment, meaning I had to ask for it. I found this difficult.

"So is it OK to pay now for your advert?" I would ask, after a lengthy conversation about the weather and such.

"Oh yeah, I almost forgot. Lucky you reminded me" they would say.

I knew straight-away who the good clients were. They had their payments ready for me to collect, all too happy to hand the money over. Then there were the few who took me for a long stroll down Guilt Lane.

"Business has been ever so slow these last few weeks. I can hardly even feed the family at the moment. Things are pretty drastic."

It was hard, but I knew I had to retain a strong mind, after all this was a business transaction and I'd kept my half of the bargain.

"Oh no, that's too bad" I would say. "You must still pay for your advert though, so that will be eighty Euros please."

Feedback from readers was equally impressive. I received a whole load of e-mails from *The Sentinel* lovers, all overjoyed to see the magazine again.

When the first issue had been delivered, it was time to make a start on the second edition for October. It was only just the beginning of September and already I was thinking of October. I thought about the time of the year, Halloween, and designed a black front cover with a bright orange pumpkin head.

Torre del Mar had reverted to normality by now. The tourists had returned to their home towns, so finding a parking space was easier again. It was still hot though, around twenty-five degrees most days, and I had an amazing golden brown tan. My parent's balcony was a brilliant sun trap and I sat there every morning collecting the rays. I was happy with my appearance; my skin was glowing and I felt healthier than I had for a long time.

"You'll get skin cancer if you're not careful" said my mother. "It's bad for your skin, you know? Gives you wrinkles."

I chose not to listen to her comments. I felt good and I looked good so that was all that mattered. I had started seeing Gavin practically every day. He loved drinking in *Bar Billard*, where I met him for the first time when my friend Nicole was over. Whenever we met there I would grin and bear the company of the regulars, most of whom would disappear into the toilets for a few minutes and reappear with glazed eyes, rubbing their noses.

My initial observation that Spain only attracted old people was untrue. As the days rolled by I met and heard about a whole stack of younger ex-pats, even some of my clients were in their late twenties or early thirties.

Although I had now met a couple of good friends, I yearned for more. In the UK I had a large group of chums, who I would meet on Friday and Saturday nights. I missed those fun evenings out (even if they were cold and rainy).

Every time I saw Gavin, his phone would ring and he would depart Earth to engage in high-pressure business-related discussions. His latest company had just launched and he channelled most his time into developing it. I felt left out and unimportant.

"You should franchise *The Sentinella*" he said one day. "You'd make an absolute killing out of it. You could sell people the rights to run *The Sentinella* in different areas of Spain. Trust me, it'd do really well, you'll be driving around in a Ferrari before you know it."

His last comment didn't surprise me. Possessions were all that really mattered to him. He lived in a totally material world. So long as he had a cool car, the latest mobile phone, a fancy watch and a penthouse apartment with a rooftop pool, he was happy. His idea of franchising the magazine was interesting, but I knew it wasn't the right time. I had only brought out one issue so I wasn't exactly an expert. There were still a whole heap of problems that needed addressing before I could help people set up a business in the same field.

"Yeah, maybe in the future" I said. "But definitely not now. I've got way too much on my plate at the moment."

"Well let me know when you're ready" said Gavin. "I could help you. We'll do it together and split the profits fifty-fifty."

I was slightly disturbed at his grand plan. 'Is he just with me because he has his greedy eyes on my business' I thought. 'Is that what all this is really about?' I swept the thoughts to the back of my mind.

The following evening Gavin took me to a really expensive restaurant, the classiest in town. We dressed to the nines. I wore a little black dress and he donned a linen suit with a beige shirt. The eatery boasted an amazing interior, chandeliers dangled from the ceiling, reflecting candlelight in a million directions, golden statues adorned the mantelpieces and exquisite pictures decorated the walls. I felt like a princess as Gavin held the door open for me and the waiter led us to our table, in a private room.

"A bottle of your finest red" said Gavin, as the smartly dressed waiter stood awaiting our drinks orders, like a cat awaiting his food. It would have been nice to have had a say, but still "finest red" sounded good.

"Ever tried Beluga Caviar?" Gavin asked. I assumed I was meant to know what it was.

"No" I said. "Caviar looks gross. Little eggs isn't it?"

"Well yes" answered Gavin. "But it tastes out of this world and Beluga is the most expensive you can get. Look, it's seventy Euros. We'll get one to share, yeah?"

I didn't want to ruin his plans with ordering the most expensive dish on the menu, so agreed. It looked disgusting, a cluster of tiny black dots, which resembled the poo of an animal. I held my breath as the first morsel entered my mouth. It certainly didn't cause my taste buds to water. I wished I had a prawn cocktail or a plate of melon instead. The bill amounted to two-hundred and eighty Euros, which I thought was way OTT for a meal destined to end up down the pan.

"Keidi, I love you" said Gavin during dessert.

I choked on my cheesecake. I couldn't help feeling his timing was a little coincidental. It was just two days ago that we had the magazine franchise chat. Maybe he had thought more about it and realised what a brilliant money-spinner it could be. Perhaps his declarations of love were attempts to reel me in, so I would agree to work in partnership with him. I wasn't stupid, but I played along with his game anyway. I was in the most powerful position, not he.

It was now the end of September and Torre del Mar had finally returned to normality as the tourists left for their home towns. I strolled along the sea front remembering the hive of activity, which was now replaced by the sound of the waves lapping the shore. Gone were the children jumping on bouncy castles and trampolines, gone were the jacket-potato sellers and gone were the street tradesmen displaying their wares. My mind ran riot over all the goings-ons of the last few months, but I was distracted by my mobile phone ringing tone.

"It's Colin's dad here" said a voice on the other end. "I'm just calling to let you know how marvellous I thought the first issue of *The Sentinella* was. You've done my son proud."

A tear clung to the corner of my eye.

"Thanks" I said. "That means such a lot to me. I'm sure Colin is up there right now with the angels, smiling down on us all."

At that moment I really believed he was.

I didn't have too long to complete the second issue of *The Sentinella* (October 2004) and found it harder to write the editorial this time around. I was overjoyed to receive my first phone call from a client wishing to place an advert. I also received more on-line support from my computer genius uncle, who gave me detailed guidelines of how to design quality colour adverts. The colour centre in my first issue looked atrocious and the advertisers weren't happy. With my uncle's help I combated the problems and produced a better colour section in the second edition.

While they were being printed I spent a few days away with Gavin. We toured the villages of Granada, staying wherever took our fancy. The road trip opened my eyes to some beautiful scenery. I saw pretty little windmills, deep gorges, gushing rivers, fields of olive trees and random goat herds. We drove all the way through the province of Granada and came out along the coast of Almería. I had such a wonderful weekend, but all that changed on the journey home.

"Keidi, I'd like to tell you something. I haven't been totally honest with you," said Gavin, stuffing a chocolate chip muffin in his mouth.

"What is it?"

"Well, there are two things actually. I really like you and I know you'll find out at some point, so I think it's best to be up front."

A stray chocolate chip clutched to his lip.

"Tell me" I said, preparing for the worst.

"Firstly, my age" he said, lapping up the choc chip.

"What?" You're not really twenty-seven?"

"No, I'm thirty-four."

I was livid. "Why did you lie to me? What was the point?"

"Well you're going out with me, aren't you? You're only twenty-three. I didn't think you'd even consider dating me if you'd known the truth."

I was angry, but chose to keep the ugly trait trapped inside. I wanted him to reveal the second part of his dishonesty too.

"Come on then" I said. "What else did you want to say?"

"I told you I just moved out here because I split up with my girlfriend in the UK; and it's not a lie, we really did break up, but there was another reason as well, a bigger reason." He looked at me briefly, for reassurance I think.

"I'm listening," I said.

In a nutshell he did some naughty things in the UK and absconded to Spain to run away. The revelation shocked me and I felt like I was going to throw up.

How was I ever going to trust this man? Life had the rotten habit of throwing some curiously stinking things into my path.

Teething Problems

I used the new father and son printer for the October issue, as there was no way I could endure the stapling ordeal again, but if it wasn't one thing it was another. This time the pages were inserted in the wrong order in half the magazines, skipping directly from page eleven to page fifteen. My Dad and I delivered the correct issues, but stress bubbled while I waited for the faulty half to be amended. When I received them, I noticed some of the colour print missing from the cover, where the staples had been hacked out and replaced.

All the deliveries had me working up an appetite and I found myself eating out more than usual. Gavin and I spent one Sunday in Nerja lunching at Burriana Beach, in the famous Ayos. Ayo is the name of one of the five boys who discovered the Nerja caves in the nineteen-fifties, while exploring, as young boys do. They squeezed through a narrow passageway almost completely blocked with fallen rock and discovered the entrance. The Nerja Caves are now a popular tourist attraction and one of the reasons the area has grown so much in recent years. Ayo, who is now an old man, has since opened his own chiringuito (beach bar) and every Sunday he cooks paella in huge frying pans to share among diners, who can eat as much as possible. His paella is extremely tasty, but I was alarmed to find pieces of rabbit in it. Bunny rabbits are kept as pets in the UK. I felt queasy at the idea of one being slaughtered and served with rice.

"I'll have yours if you're gonna leave it" said Gavin, helping himself to my lumps of rabbit meat. "I don't know why you don't eat it though. Rabbit is a traditional ingredient of paella, there's nothing weird about it. It tastes real good, a bit like chicken actually."

He was welcome to it!

Another of my down and depressed spells surfaced. It was frustrating knowing my apartment was still sitting there empty, but I couldn't move in. The horror stories I had heard about the Spanish electricity company were true. I had waited five months yet it still wasn't connected. Without electricity, I couldn't have a kitchen fitted either. I imagined still living with my parents when I was fifty-odd.

"Don't worry darling" my now white-haired mother would say, sitting in her rocking chair knitting. "Maybe tomorrow."

Seven months living with my parents was taking its toll and I felt like my life had no real purpose. My row-ometer frequently hit ten and full-scale arguments erupted. Desperate to make some more friends, I added a small article in the magazine asking if they were any youngsters wanting to meet others. I didn't anticipate any response, but was pleasantly surprised to receive an e-mail from a girl called Zoe, who had just moved in with her parents, at Lake Viñuela. The lake area is one of the most picturesque regions of the Axarquia, and easily accessible as the main road from Torre del Mar leads there. Small villages are scattered around it, including Alcaucín, Puente don Manuel, La Viñuela, Periana, Triana and Benamargosa to name but a few.

"Hiya, sorry I'm late" she said, collapsing into the chair next to me.

"My bloody four-year-old wouldn't let me go. She was crying 'mummy, mummy, please don't leave me'!"

"No worries," I said. "I don't have kids so I've no idea what it's like."

"Keep it that way if I were you. At times they aren't worth the hassle."

I noticed that Zoe had a chin and nose stud, plus a couple of tattoos. She wore loud, chunky jewellery. I liked her hippy style, and she radiated energy. We really hit it off, considering that we had been strangers just three hours before. She asked me about the magazine and I told her about Gavin. She spoke about her ex-boyfriend and her daughter.

"Just fancied a change," she said when I asked why she had moved to Spain

"But I can't stand living back with my parents. God, they do my head in. I feel like a teenager again."

Hallelujah! I had something in common with this girl. It was liberating to share the way I felt with someone who had the same feelings. I had started to feel alone in this world, but Zoe helped me to remain sane.

"So tell me more about Gavin" she asked. "Is he the one? Church bells ringing?"

"Definitely not. He's just someone to go out with. It's lonely here and he gets me out my parent's skin."

"Well, we can meet whenever you like" said Zoe. "I'll be wanting to go out lots, so there's no need for you to feel lonely any more."

"Cool" I said.

Zoe was different to the type of friend I hung out with in the UK, but she was more than welcome in my life.

On the morning of November the sixth, the phone rang at around four in the morning, waking my parents and I. Dad answered the call. I smiled as I lay there. It was the date I had predicted that my sister's baby girl would be born. Charli Knight was born at nine twenty-two am in Medway Hospital, Gillingham, weighing seven pounds nine ounces. My mum was in tears at the news.

"I can't be there for her" she said through drenched eyes. "This is one of the most important days of her life and I'm stuck here, miles away. I feel so useless."

Needless to say, my parents fled back to the UK so they could admire their first grandchild and help their daughter out. They hauled a whole suitcase of gifts with them.

My twenty fourth Birthday was fast approaching and due to the lack of friends, I had to sweep together everyone I knew to try and make the evening a memorable one. I envisaged scraping burnt scrambled egg from the bottom of a frying pan. I invited Sarah and her brother Rob, Zoe (who brought her sister), and Gavin. We hung out in some Nerja bars and as usual Gavin talked non-stop about himself and how great his life was.

"I've just moved from my penthouse apartment in Algarrobo Costa to a four bedroom fully furnished deluxe apartment near Torre. It's top notch, seriously. The lounge is gigantic and there's everything imaginable. I'm really happy there."

I sat there wondering "why?" for most of the night. Sarah looked like she was having the worst night of her night. Rob seemed uncomfortable too, especially when Zoe and her sister smashed glasses on the floor for no apparent reason.

"What would you say if I asked you to marry me" whispered Gavin out the blue, slurring his words like an old drunk. My rum and coke slipped down the wrong hole and I erupted into a coughing fit.

"Won't be a sec" I called back as I sped to the Ladies, dragging Sarah with me.

"He just asked what I'd say if he proposed. I really don't like him enough to marry him."

"Look, Keidi, it's your life, but he's not the kind of man I can see you ending up with. You can do so much better."

The next day was my actual Birthday and I awoke feeling miserable. Birthdays were meant to be happy occasions, but I felt the opposite. Gavin called early.

"Hey princess, Happy Birthday! How do you fancy coming shopping so I can buy you a present?"

I was disappointed, having hoped for a surprise that he had taken the effort to choose. Instead he 'put' me in a couple of my favourite clothes shops and told me to find some I liked. It didn't cross my mind right then that many men find it difficult choosing presents for women. Rather than appreciating his generosity, which was his way of showing me he cared, I reacted with dismay. In essence, I was acting like an ungrateful bitch. Later, we met outside a rather shabby and 'cheap' restaurant, which happened to be located directly under his apartment. 'What became of chandeliers, finest red and Beluga Caviar?' I wondered, as I shoved lukewarm salami pizza into my mouth. After dinner an argument brewed.

"Would you mind dropping me home tonight?" I asked. Home (currently still my parent's apartment) was only a twenty minute walk away, but I was tired and my feet hurt, plus I wanted to check that he cared about me. After a disappointing Birthday it was my way of finding out.

"You're having a laugh aren't you? It's only round the corner, you lazy cow!" He was half serious, half joking.

"Well that's nice, on my Birthday as well" I said. "You're a really fantastic boyfriend some times."

"Well if you're going to be like that I'll take back those clothes I bought you earlier" he said with a raised voice.

"You can walk home tonight, exercise is good for you anyway."

"Then forget about helping me with the magazine. I'll do it myself."

That was the moment I saw the real Gavin break through. His whole face changed shape, but it was too late. The words had already left my mouth.

"Right that's it! Get out of my flat. Just like all the others you are. Dunno why I expected any different. Get out. Go on…"

I met him with resistance, so he grabbed my legs and tried pulling me out as if I was a hysterical animal. I clung to whatever furniture I could find to mar his attempts. I wasn't asking him for a twenty-four carat diamond ring or an all-inclusive trip to Barbados; just a lift home. I really couldn't see what the problem was. Things were never the same between us after that row. Regardless, it wasn't the ideal way to end my apparently special day.

While my relationship with Gavin was turning to dust, things were looking up in another area of my life. The electricity had finally been connected in my apartment and the carpenters had even made a start on the kitchen. I commissioned a Spanish carpenter called Antonio to fit it upon the recommendation of friends of my parents. I chose pine units with silver handles and a dark marble surface. Antonio suggested a design, then got to work with his colleagues measuring, chopping and fitting. A month later it was finished and I started filling the cupboards with crockery and cutlery. Communicating with Antonio and his team was difficult. I was attempting to learn Spanish by reading children's books and listening to TV shows, but it wasn't as easy as I had believed. Usually I had to resort to hand actions and pointing, but the message usually registered in the end.

"Estoy caliente" I said one sunny morning. The carpenters looked at each other and laughed. I thought I had told them I was hot.

"Qué?" I asked. The men were in hysterics, laughing so much they couldn't even speak to tell me what was so funny. I later found out via a friend that to say *estoy caliente* literally means I am hot and in Spain this has sexual connotations, basically meaning 'I am horny.' Now I understood! The correct way would be to say *hace calor* meaning it is hot or *tengo calor* for I am hot (in the temperature sense). One day when discussing the amount of drawers I wanted, I made another error.

"Quiero tres cojones."

"Cojones?" asked Antonio, laughing. "Esta es una palabra muy mala."

A bad word? Whoops! I looked in the dictionary and learnt that *cojones* are part of the male reproductive organs.

"Lo siento. Cajones," I said "Cojones, no!"

It was all too easy for us *Guiris* (foreigners) to make disconcerting blunders on the language front.

To take my attention away from Gavin, I arranged a trip back to the UK, my first visit in eight months. I arranged to stay with my sister, who was now also a mother. I couldn't wait to see her and baby Charli. Seeing the tiny bundle of life planted the thought of whether I wanted a baby one day. They looked like hard work. The living room appeared as if a bomb had hit. Everywhere I glanced there were baby items; a cot, musical rocking chairs, nappies, wipes, lotions, soft toys, rattles and tiny clothes. Nonetheless, I learnt how to hold and feed a baby, plus how to change a nappy. I felt an incredible wave of peace as I held baby Charli and rocked her to sleep. Not surprisingly, the weather was freezing so I didn't venture out much, choosing to remain indoors in front of English television and central heating. The trip made a nice change, but I couldn't wait to return to warmer climes.

I didn't miss Gavin one crumb, so I knew I had to break up with him pretty sharply. He was playing havoc with my head and continuing a relationship with him would be pointless. I texted him. 'Sorry but I don't feel our relationship is working so would like to finish it.' He answered immediately, with 'OK'. Clearly he didn't want me to know that he cared; if he did, I mean. I reminisced about our time together and decided that despite the revelations and lies Gavin was a pretty good egg. I knew that the way I interpreted his help with franchising *The Sentinella* was only a reflection of my own insecurities. Looking back, I realised that he was genuinely trying to help.

For the December 2004 issue I found a great cover shot of snowflakes and added the clever line, 'Snow chance of this here!' My parents returned to the UK a week before Christmas and they weren't flying back to Spain until the beginning of January. They were worried that I would feel lonely away from the family over the season of goodwill.

"There's a big bag of presents for you in your bedroom" said my Mum as she kissed me goodbye. "Don't open them until Christmas Day!"

I didn't feel I deserved any gifts after my behaviour of late. All I seemed to do around my parents was pick arguments with them and be miserable. I knew the rows were just my way of coping with personal issues. It's a well-known fact that people always take out their grievances on those closest to them. The big bag of presents showed me that they weren't taking my current mood swings to heart, which made me feel slightly better.

When I delivered the December issue of *The Sentinella* to Fit Nick's accountancy office, he gave me two kisses and a huge bear hug.

"Have a good one" he said, squeezing the air out my lungs. "Maybe we could go for a drink some time? I'm never so busy over the Christmas period."

"Sure" I said, as if the proposition didn't bother me either way. "Text me."

Really, I still fancied him like hell.

I had become well known to the businesses in Torre del Mar. There were English businesses opening left, right and centre. The ex-pat community was widening as wise people cottoned on to the niche in the market for goods and services that us Brits needed and missed.

A new British food shop had recently opened and the owner was extremely helpful, advising me on other businesses about to open. There was also a luxury gift shop and a ladies clothes shop opening that month and I sold advertising space to both of them. Whereas the black and white pages of the magazine sold effortlessly, the colour centre proved more difficult. Only one of the original colour adverts, from the first issue had stayed in. The others had all dropped out and I needed adverts to replace them with.

Spending Christmas alone like a little old lady was a bigger issue than the difficulty of selling colour advertisements, so imagine my delight when Sarah invited me to spend it with her and her family. On Christmas Eve I stayed the night in their house, which sat forty minutes up a mountain. On the big day we sank mulled wine while gifts were dished out left right and centre.

For the Spanish, Christmas Eve is known as *nochebuena* (the good night). Family members congregate to feast and rejoice around nativity scenes, called *Belén*, found in most homes. Essentially it's just another excuse for a good old knees up. Christmas trees and fancy lights are a more recent sight, which more and more homes now boast. Additionally the Spanish celebrate Three King's Day. On the fifth of January, *La Noche de Reyes*, people go to see *Las Caravanas de Reyes* and the 'Kings' throw sweets for the crowds. It is believed that is when the three wise men, Melchor, Gaspar and Baltasar, gave their gifts to baby Jesus. That night the children have to go to bed early, or the Kings won't appear. Shoes (not stockings) are filled with straw or barley for the tired camels, who must carry their riders throughout the night. On the morning of the sixth of January the straw has gone; replaced with presents if the child has been good. If the child has been naughty he or she receives coal. In the olden days this was real coal, but now it is made of sugar.

Traditional Christmas treats include *turrón* (a type of almond nougat) which comes in many different flavours, and a sugar-frosted fruit-filled ring called *Roscón*, which is served for breakfast on Three Kings Day. Inside one piece, someone receives a small plastic toy, rather like the English tradition of a coin inside a Christmas pudding. Whoever finds it is said to enjoy good luck throughout the rest of the year. All in all, the entire Christmas period lasts much longer than in the UK, where we celebrate on the twenty-fifth then hit the sales on Boxing Day.

"Do you fancy coming snowboarding with me?" said Rob when Sarah and her parents had gone to bed. "I've been before so I can teach you the ropes."

The glory of living on the Costa del Sol is that you have everything you could possibly want within driving distance. If you want the beach and the sea it is on your doorstep, if you prefer the mountains, zoom five minutes inland and you reach some, or if you seek snow, an hour and a half's drive time brings you to the Sierra Nevada, the ski resort of southern Spain. It is possible to spend the morning sunbathing on the beach and swimming in the sea, and the afternoon skiing or building snowmen.

"That would be cool," I said. "When's good for you?"

"Any time really," said Rob. "Let's keep an eye on the weather forecast and head up there when fresh snow has fallen. It'll be better for boarding then."

"OK, ring me when you think it would be a good day," I said.

He shuffled uncomfortably in his chair and looked at me for a moment before downing the rest of his drink.

"I'm going to bed," he said, but before leaving he planted a huge kiss on my lips and hugged me tightly. My body leapt into shock mode. I hadn't realised before but I fancied Rob, even if he did baffle me a tad.

After Christmas I met fit Nick the accountant. I had fancied the pants off him for months and finally he asked me out for a drink. I was so nervous beforehand that I downed almost half a bottle of peach schnapps. We chatted a lot and as the evening wore on Nick ordered me shots of various strong drinks. When we finally retreated he kissed me goodbye. This was no ordinary kiss, but the passionate full-on variety. I went to bed that night with my insides dancing. Maybe Nick had fancied me for ages, like I had fancied him? I wondered whether anything would come of the kiss.

I slept for most the next day thinking about the year gone by, so much had happened. I looked forward to the coming one, as I sensed that good times lay ahead.

Mr Money texted me out the blue asking if I was still looking for a job. I had great pleasure in revealing that I was now a magazine Editor and owner so I didn't need his job. Boy that felt good. I felt like adding "so kiss my arse" to the message, but refrained myself.

New Year's Eve (*Nochevieja*) came and fit Nick didn't bother inviting me out with him and his pals. Instead I spent the evening with Rob, who texted asking what I was up to. His sister Sarah was back in the UK for the week and he was obviously lonely. I wore a red bra and knickers set, as apparently it is a trend amongst the Spanish and said to bring luck throughout the year. I went the extra mile and made sure my two-piece was also sexy, just in case Rob happened to see it. During the night I realised that Rob was a splendid mixture of things. Physically speaking he was manly, fit and attractive and on the inside he was considerate, kind, warm, deep, thoughtful and a little strange. I didn't mind the strange aspect, as I felt like we had something in common. I fancied him like mad as we stood in Nerja square, surrounded by partying masses and exploding fireworks. Throughout the night I wanted him to draw me close, or take my hand, but he didn't.

"Hello Keidi, how about a photo," said an advertising client standing in front of us pointing a camera at our heads. "Is that your boyfriend? A good choice if I may say so."

My face went the colour of a tomato.

At midnight small bags of grapes were handed out to the crowds. It is a Spanish tradition to gobble twelve, one every five seconds during the last minute before midnight.

"I can't fit any more in," I said giggling with a mouthful of grape pulp.

In the New Year my Dad drove my hugely missed Ford Ka from the UK to Torre del Mar, which meant I could *finally* move into my apartment. I was ever so excited. It couldn't have arrived at a better time; a new year, a new start, and all that...

On The Slopes

The brink of the New Year felt fresh and welcome, heralding a new chapter in my life.

Now that I had a car and my kitchen was fitted, I could finally move into my apartment. I felt relieved to have my own space again. At last I could eat when I wanted, cook what I wanted, watch TV when I wanted and sleep when I wanted. The novelty wore off after one week when the bad weather reared its ugly head. Most weekends I sat in front of my laptop listening to the rain and wishing I had more friends. I even craved the company of my parents again and found myself visiting them on numerous occasions. That old case of 'you don't know what you've got until its gone'.

Despite the miserable outlook, I spent at least one night a week out, usually in the company of Sarah and her brother. I felt awkward around Rob. My eye would meet his and I wouldn't know where to look.

My man-pulling aura, which had been shining so brightly while Nicole visited, was fading and now that I had split up with Gavin I needed a booster again. I wanted a man in my life. It sounds a little desperate, but I felt I needed one. Brilliant timing, as Rob called one day like a bolt out the darkness.

"Hi Keidi, it's Rob here. What are you up to?"

"Hiya" I said, trying to stay cool, but feeling far from it. "I've just pulled up in Torre del Mar."

"Great!" he said. "I'm in Torre too. Do you fancy going for a bite to eat somewhere?"

The events of the last few months had all led up to this. The unexpected kiss and hug around Christmas, inviting me snowboarding, New Year's Eve in Nerja and now this, calling me in the middle of the day to 'do lunch'. Surely this meant something. Typically and somewhat annoyingly, I had already arranged to meet my writer friend, Anna.

"I'm sorry" I said. "I'm meeting Anna, but you can join us. Anna won't mind."

During lunch Rob spoke more about snowboarding, asking me when I could go. In the back of my mind I remembered fit Nick the accountant had said the same. I loved the thought of snowboarding with Rob above anything else, but I knew I would be a bundle of nerves. I wasn't strong enough to cope. When Rob left, Anna and I spoke about him.

"I can't work out if he fancies you or not" she said. "He seems to be giving out mixed signals; maybe he doesn't know himself." I respected Anna's opinion, as she was in her early thirties so clearly wiser than me.

In the meantime I needed to sort out insurance for my red Ford Ka. The experience was rather hellish, as Spanish companies don't like to insure people under the age of twenty-five and for another ten months I was only twenty-four. Also, my car had English plates which becomes illegal three months after arrival of the car into Spain. My battle to acquire car insurance began with me ringing around fifteen different insurers, both English and Spanish. At last one said:

"Yes we insure twenty-four year olds, but only if you're female. We can't insure cars with English plates, only Spanish. Sorry."

Finally, I insured my car in England. I knew it wasn't legal in Spain, but it made me feel better knowing I had some form of cover. Besides, there was always the green card, which I could acquire for limited time frames when I felt more accident-prone. I also enquired about the cost of changing my English number-plates to Spanish, but almost keeled over when I heard the figure was a thousand Euros. That was more than my flagging '97 Ka was worth! I decided I would rather risk getting caught and paying a fine.

Driving on the right hand side made sense to me. I wondered how I had ever coped on the left. My driving improved ten-fold within a relatively short time and I even mastered a reverse park. With my car now in use I didn't have to rely on my father to ferry me around. I began visiting clients alone, to collect payments, take down new advert details and distribute magazines. My confidence flourished and I even engaged in some cold calling. If the business owners said "no", I didn't let their rejection bother me. If they said "yes", I felt an amazing sense of achievement.

I had to deal with problematic clients too. I was certainly learning a packet of new skills. Now and again clients would reserve an advert space then contact me a few days before the magazine was due to go to print and try to cancel it.

"I'm sorry but it's too late to cancel," I would tell them. "I've reserved a space for you and as such haven't tried selling it elsewhere. You must have it at this stage."

Then there were the payment collections. I think some clients liked the power of keeping me waiting for half an hour or telling me to return four times before finally presenting the cash. People in general really starting getting on my wick. I managed to stay sane with the sound knowledge that my profits were rising every month and as such my bank balance was also building up.

After all the snowboarding banter with Rob, I finally went with Nick. He called me out the blue one evening to see if I could go the very next morning.

"Uhm. Err. Yeah, why not?" I said.

"Great!" said Nick. "Meet me at Lake Viñuela at seven in the morning."

I spared a thought for Rob, but knew I couldn't refuse a day on the slopes with fit Nick. He was so decisive and that was sexy. Rob pigeon-footed around making a lot of suggestions, but he never actually took a bite.

The journey to the Sierra Nevada was most picturesque and as I studied the distant mountains I thought how they resembled the dessert, tiramisu. I imagined tucking into a giant portion, the same size as the distant mountains and my stomach groaned.

Sierra Nevada translates as Snowy Mountains. The fascinating and most popular mountain range for skiing in Spain is situated in the Granada province, in the Alpujarras. It contains the highest point of mainland Spain, Mulhacen, which stands at three-thousand, four-hundred and seventy nine metres. As we left the car I was almost blinded by the brightness, caused by the sunlight reflecting off a gleaming blanket of pure white. The chill-factor, coupled with warm sunshine, was a unique mix. There were many people skiing, from small children to elderly couples, all taking no shame in toppling over frequently like 'first steps' babies. They wore thick ski-suits with woolly hats, gloves and sunglasses. Nick boasted about how great he was at snowboarding.

"I go at least five times a year and I've got all the top gear and about five different boards" he said.

"Well as long as you don't leave me at the top, while you race down."

Nick laughed.

"Nah, I wouldn't do that. But while you're having a lesson, I'll probably do a couple of red runs."

Nick helped me tie my ski-boots and step into the body-suit, before we caught a chairlift to the snow area. On the way up I gulped, as through the glass I could see lots of skiers and snowboarders toppling over.

"Wow! That looks cool," I said, pointing at a rapid sledge pulled along by dogs. I want a go on one of them." Nick laughed again.

"They're only for people who are injured on the slopes" he said. "That's like the ambulance. It takes people to the medical centre for treatment."

"Oh, OK. Never mind then."

At the top I stepped out on to thick snow. I liked the crunching sound it made as we trudged through, leaving our individual footprints. Nick took me to the nursery slopes to await my lesson.

"Right, I'll leave you here then" he said. "I'm going to do a red run."

With that he whisked off, before I could call after him to stop. I was a little annoyed that he had left me. He could have at least waited until I was called for my lesson. As I waited I realised how uncomfortable I felt. I was weighed down with heavy clothes, snow-boots and board, plus I was freezing and my cheeks stung with the cold. Ten minutes later a foreign lady in the official Sierra Nevada uniform approached me.

"Hi. I'm your instructor" she said in bad, broken English. "Follow me pleaz."

The lesson was useful but I didn't feel like I learnt a great deal. All I remember was the instructor screaming "back on your heelz, back on your heelz," as I slid along the snow, usually ending up on my bum.

"You must stay on your heelz" she reiterated. "This iz what helps you balance, you understand?"

"Yes" I said, hauling myself up again. "Just a little difficult, you know, first time and all that."

After thirty minutes practising balancing by shifting my weight "back on my heelz" the lesson was over.

"I hope it was useful" said the instructor before leaving for her next candidate.

"No" I thought. "Actually, not." I stood on the sidelines and waited for Bloody Nick to return. Twenty minutes later he turned up.

"How did it go?" he asked. "You feel ready to hit the slopes yet? We can start with a yellow run, that's the easiest."

"OK" I said, like a lost little girl. We took a chairlift even higher into the mountains, but we had to board this one as it moved.

"It's easy," Nick said. "Just watch me and do the same, but try to be quick."

My leg jammed into a funny position and my arms locked awkwardly around my board. The other end was the hard part.

"We have to jump off when I say go" said Nick. "Just try to stay on your feet." Easy for him to say, Mr Expert Snowboarder of the Century.

"Go!" he yelled. Nick landed on the snow perfectly, while I froze in my seat.

"Keidi? You're meant to follow me. Quick, now!"

I panicked and lunged off the chairlift, landing in an uncompromising position, with one leg bent at a one-hundred and eighty degree angle under my body and the other splayed out at the side. Bloody Nick was in hysterics.

"Ow! Help. My leg is stuck. I can't move." He helped me up and I felt stupid for the second time that day.

"Right now watch and learn" he said, as he sped off down the slope. "Look how I move my body to turn."

I wasn't interested in how he moved his body, I just wanted to reach the bottom and it seemed a long way down. After landing in the bushes on the sidelines a couple of times and almost flooring a little boy, I finally grasped the skill.

"This is easy" I screamed as I reeled down the slope. "Who said snowboarding was hard?"

At the bottom we stopped for a baguette and drink. I chose wine. I had almost finished it when Nick piped up.

"You'll be drunk when you've finished that. The altitude makes people get drunk quicker you know? I'm going to do a couple of black runs now, you practise the yellow, then we can meet again in half an hour and try a green together. How does that sound?"

"See you in half hour" I said as I approached the moving chair lift once more. I stood for a while simply watching it move, my head fuzzy after the wine.

'Ah, the fresh air, the blinding snow, the...' Bang! A chair from behind collided with the side of my head, just above my eye. I fell to the ice, only just managing to slither out the way of the next one. My head pounded like a hat of steel had been placed upon it. The chair lift operator dashed over to see if I was OK.

"Si, si" I said "No problema."

He helped me into the next chair and I set off on my journey to the top. I kept a close look out for the point where Nick had jumped off before. This time I leapt just on-time and despite my head spinning from a glass of wine and a knock, I didn't even fall over. At the bottom of the slope I hung around for Nick.

"Fancy trying a green one now?" He asked. "Think we'll have to make this the last though. I'm shattered. Could do with heading back soon." Just when I was getting into it!

"Yeah, sure" I said. At the top I couldn't see that it looked much different from the yellow run.

"It's a lot steeper" Nick said. "So you'll go faster."

"Well that's OK" I said. "I like going fast."

He was right, too. When we set off I raced along like a tiger chasing a deer. I had no idea what I was doing. It was just pure fluke that I managed to stay on two feet for more than ten seconds at a time.

"Wow! Go girl" shouted Nick as he performed a show-off spin in mid-air to remind me that he was better.

I deliberately upped the pace, gathering even more speed. Then disaster struck. I lost my balance and landed with my left arm twisted behind my back a few hundred metres further towards the bottom of the run. Nick dashed over.

"My God, are you OK? That was some fall." I lay face down in the snow, not moving a muscle.

"No actually. Not OK" I said. "I think I've broken my arm. It really hurts. I can't move it." Nick helped me to my feet.

"Owwww," I screamed as my arm moved with my body.

"I think it's sprained" said Nick. "Often that hurts more than a breakage. Can you make it the rest of the way down the slope?"

"No" I said, in agony. My whole body was shaking from the shock and I felt sick, and to make matters worse I weed myself as I fell. I didn't tell Nick that small fact, but I could feel the wetness in my knickers. It was a good job my trousers were waterproof!

"OK, wait here" he said. "I'm going to fetch help." He returned with the sledge ambulance, which I had my eye on earlier in the day.

"Hop on" said the driver, taking my snowboard. The ride was a dangerous one. I nearly fell off several times, as we flew over lumps and bumps, avoiding skiers with sharp twists and turns. We arrived at a medical room where some doctors greeted me.

"Sign your name here please" one said, handing me a pen and gesturing to a form. My hand was shaking so much that I couldn't even hold the pen properly.

"Tranquila" said a male doctor.

He prepared a needle for an injection. I hoped it contained something to relax me. My heart was still beating hard and I felt faint. The doctors X-rayed my arm and confirmed it was badly sprained. They wrapped it in a bandage and hung it in a sling. Nick appeared and said we would head back. My car was still outside Nick's office and I couldn't drive, so I called my saviour Dad to collect me, who came to the rescue yet again. He was a supportive soul and it was all too easy to take advantage of his good nature at times. I hated having to ask him such favours, as at twenty-four I should have been taking control of my own life, not relying on him at every slip-up. As I lay in bed that night a mixture of thoughts flowed through my head. One thing was certain; I had chosen the wrong man to go snowboarding with.

The next day I expected a phone call from Nick to see how I was, but I heard not a peep. In fact I didn't hear from him until a week later when he sent a text. 'I've fallen in love with a girl and it feels amazing, just thought I should let you know.' I couldn't believe Nick's audacity. He didn't even ask how my arm was!

Preparing *The Sentinella* April 2005 issue was a lot more difficult than I had expected. I was thankful I had two arms, but wished I could use both, which spurred me to write about the snow-boarding ordeal. I felt liberated writing about my personal experiences in the monthly editorial, which would be read by more than three-thousand people. It was almost like self-counselling. Writing about what had happened, helped me to let go and see the occurrences from a different and often funny perspective. It was rather like a blog on paper and readers would often comment on my life. Sometimes I felt this was a little strange and I would be lost for words. It was easy to forget that strangers knew more about my life than some of my closest friends.

Bloody Nick turned up in a bar at Lake Viñuela, a week after sending me the text, to rub salt into the wound.

"It was love at first sight you know?" he told me, looking thoroughly smitten. I wondered why he went out of his way to make me feel stupid.

As it transpired, the relationship with 'the love of his life' lasted just one month, which made me feel better. He received his comeuppance from the powers of the universe. I was beginning to realise how the world worked, and it interested me.

Copy Cats

My writer friend Anna revealed over lunch that a magazine was launching in the mountains, almost identical to *The Sentinella*.

"The first issue is due out in May 05" she said. "From what I can gather, it's going to be exactly the same size as *The Sentinella*, with black and white pages and a colour centre. All the adverts are going to be the same size, too, it seems."

The news made me leave the comfy seat I had chosen to relax on, and make *The Sentinella* big. I couldn't stomach the thought of a rival copycat magazine becoming fatter than *The Sentinella*. The copycats would soon learn who was boss in this game.

"I shouldn't worry too much though" said Anna. "I mean, competition is healthy and it only means you're doing a good thing if people choose to copy. They're a young family who want to make a living just like you, remember."

At the time I couldn't see it, but my wise friend had a mighty fine point. Now I have accepted that competition is indeed a fact of life and that everyone with a good idea is copied eventually. I only had to look at McDonalds and Burger King or Pizza Hut and Pizza Express. One of them must have opened before the other and who can blame a young family for starting another magazine in a growing area, which is hardly touched in terms of advertising. Decent jobs are so hard to come by, that using one's initiative is necessary and now I look at what I once saw as 'the copycats' and instead view them as 'intelligent'.

In the meantime my ex-flatmate, Jo, came to visit for a week and she was all prepared for sightseeing. Jo is a shy Malaysian girl, an accountant who despised her colleagues as they made her feel extremely unwelcome in the office. I knew Jo could do with the trip and she had never been to Spain before. I looked forward to showing her around.

"It's not very green, is it?" she said, as her eyes scanned dusty roadsides with no grass and straw-like trees.

"Well spotted" I said.

"But it's very mountainous" she continued, looking ahead into the yonder. "I had no idea Spain had so many mountains. What's the highest here, do you know?"

Jo was very intellectual and lapped up knowledge and facts like a hungry tree frog. I was ashamed to admit that I didn't have a clue.

"I only live here" I said laughing. "How on earth am I supposed to know the answer to a question like that? I just about know where to find Spain on the world map, let alone the name of its highest mountain."

During her stay Jo encouraged me to join her on a sightseeing extravaganza in Málaga City. We started with the Roman Theatre and after getting shouted at for standing on a bit we weren't meant to, we swiftly moved on to the neighbouring Alcazaba fortress. The Alcazaba was built in the eleventh century and there were three parts; the patio of the fountains, the court of the orange trees; and the pond area. I really enjoyed exploring all of them, and there are some breathtaking views over the city. Two hours and two sunburnt noses later we moved on to the Castillo de Gibralfo, an Arab castle built during the fourteenth century. Walking here was not an easy task, especially in the heat of the afternoon sun. We followed a long uphill path and the route completely knackered me. I almost kissed the man at the top selling water! Our last adventure of the day was spent at the Plaza de Toros (bull ring). There was a small museum with various odds and ends, including stuffed bull heads, the clothes of famous bull fighters and nasty pictures of injuries acquired as a result of the sport.

Other places we visited included the marina at La Herradura and the Nerja Caves. The marina is located twenty minutes along the coast east of Nerja on the Costa Tropical, the coastline of Granada. It is a smaller, quieter and calmer version of Puerto Banus and it's possible to walk full-circle around the entire area, stopping to view expensive boutiques and yachts of all shapes and sizes. Most of the yachts found here are small, but they still look stunning as their sails flap in the breeze.

"That one's mine" I said pointing at one called *The Jolly Dolly*. My beady eye was particularly drawn to the sun lounge at the rear.

"And that one's mine" said Jo laughing and pointing at the largest in the marina.

La Herradura Marina is framed neatly by mountains, and the scenery is out of this world. It is clear that the area is well maintained by people with a keen eye for quality, and flowering plantations thrive at every nook and cranny.

"This is sooo relaxing" said Jo as we sat at a marina fronted café sipping cold drinks with views to die for.

We also spent a morning at the Nerja Caves, which are actually located in Maro, a tiny village a stones throw east of Nerja.

Containing the world's largest known stalactite, as well as a package of other archaeological treats, the caves are well worth a gander.

"Wow! It's really huge" said Jo as she took a multitude of photos of the largest stalactite hanging from the ceiling and touching the floor. Deep-purple hues and musty oranges reflected the light, creeping in via tiny holes in the roof and walls. The colours give the caves a sense of mystery and elegance. They are now used as a natural theatre where concerts and shows are staged throughout the summer.

Another day we visited Benalmádena Pueblo, which is such a contrast from the Blackpool style coastal resort. The pueblo is a beautiful place, still very Spanish, and there are some eye-opening sights to see. Firstly, and somewhat bizarrely, there is an elevator in the middle of the village, casually sitting next to a street light. I always thought elevators belonged in shopping precincts. There is also a fairytale style castle, built in memory of Christopher Columbus, full of gushing fountains, bubbling babbles and various other delights. Jo left Spain with a full digital camera and some (hopefully) fond memories.

Back to work! Having injected effort into increasing the thickness of *The Sentinella*, I was dead chuffed with the immediate results. The May issue increased by four colour pages, boosting the magazine to forty-four pages in total.

"Why don't you start selling colour adverts to other businesses rather than just estate agents?" suggested my Mum. "There might be some restaurants or other companies who want colour publicity."

I took her advice and sold colour adverts to a swimming pool shop, furniture shop, a kitchen shop, a restaurant and even a currency exchange company in the UK.

The black and white adverts were increasing too. I could barely squeeze them all in and considered boosting the black and white pages by four. This was only the beginning. I knew good things were poised to happen, I could feel it in the air. I had smelt the sweet scent of success and I wanted more. The word about *The Sentinella* was spreading, clients were receiving calls and positive feedback from their adverts and I was hearing good comments from everyone about how much they enjoyed the magazine. Readers especially loved the funny jokes I included each month. Clients introduced me to new clients, who in turn introduced me to yet more clients. It was a domino effect.

There were yet more English businesses opening in Torre del Mar too. That month a pottery café, an Irish bar and a card shop were among the newbies. The area was changing and in my mind for the better. Even though more English businesses were opening, which would no doubt attract more Brits to the area, I was happy with the type of people behind these businesses. Aside from the sports bars and greasy-spoon cafes, a greetings card shop and a pottery café were two examples of the arrival of contrasting and creative businesses. People had some dead impressive ideas and the brave ones weren't afraid to run the risk of trying.

Now that I lived in El Morche I was just up the road from Torrox Costa, which meant I could concentrate more on selling advertising space in this area, as Torre del Mar was pretty much stitched up already. Torrox Costa proved to be a tapestry of potential advertisers and gradually I won their trust. Torrox was originally a very German area, but that trend was changing. The Brits were invading, so to speak, and the German businesses were gradually being outnumbered by their British counterparts. However, along with all the advertising sales, some clients were real time-wasters and many used me during quiet spells to off-load their problems. Some days I returning home feeling like a loaded shopping bag.

Hippy chick Zoe called one day with excitement in her voice. She asked if I could meet her in the café by the lighthouse as she had some important news. I was really busy delivering the May issue, but I found a spare half an hour for a friend with gossip.

"I've got a new boyfriend" she said, as she flung her arms around my neck from behind and delivered the customary kiss on each cheek.

"Excellent" I said, trying to sound as enthusiastic as she was. "Who is it? Anyone I know?"

"Actually, yes" she said. "You know him very well. It's Nick."

Bloody Nick. I might have guessed. Nick and Zoe made the perfect pair. I think Zoe half expected me to be jealous or angry with her, given my past with him, but I wasn't. In fact I felt happy for them.

The Sentinella was becoming more and more popular but the printing quality was still not up to scratch and some clients were concerned. Coincidentally Gavin called me for the first time since I told him our relationship was over.

"Hiya, How are you?" asked Gavin.

"OK" I said. "Just fed up with bad printers. I can't seem to find a decent one."

"Really?" said Gavin. "Well I'm getting some magazines printed for my new business, so do you fancy coming around Málaga with me so we can find a decent one? They might even do us a discount."

I was a little freaked out that Gavin had called with such a proposal at this timely moment.

"Cool" I said. "When do you want to go?"

The next day we met early. It was odd to see him again after all this time, but as suspected I wasn't attracted to him. My mind had moved on and that was a relief. Gavin drove straight to an industrial estate he knew. We skimmed along, peering at all the signs to see what businesses were there.

"I reckon there'll be one just up here round this corner" said Gavin. He had this strange knack of knowing where places were.

"There, there!" I said pointing at a warehouse full of printing presses and boxes of papers. The printer's fee was so cheap it meant I could print more magazines for the same price as the previous print run.

One of my advertisers was a medium named Vicki and she booked a three-month stint to advertise her psychic powers. She asked if I could write her an editorial in return for a free reading. At the time I was feeling a little up and down. Despite the growth of *The Sentinella* I couldn't work out if I actually liked living in Spain or not. Everything was so different than what I was used to. I had changed hugely, and perhaps only for the better, but I felt lost. I didn't know if I was heading in the right direction, if I was on the right path, or even if I actually enjoyed life any more. I was confused and I knew I needed some guidance. I am very open to mediums and the spiritual world, and a strong believer, so I welcomed Vicki's proposal.

She invited me to her house and led me into her surprisingly ordinary living room. I expected to see tarot cards, crystal balls and candles, but saw nothing more than an ordinary bowl of fruit and a selection of family photos. Vicki told me how she was introduced to the world of spiritualism at the age of ten by her parents, who were members of a circle. Her reading was spot on.

"You need to pull up the blinds and let in the light and not to be scared of the bad" she said. "We must all go through the bad in life to experience the good, including you." She paused for a moment and an alarmed expression fell on to her face.

"There's someone coming in" she said. "Someone on the other side who wants to pass a message on to you. His name is Tom."

I had a granddad called Tom whom I had never known. He died just after the Second World War, when my father was only two.

"This is a well-dressed man" she said, touching her neck as she spoke. "There's something around his neck. I can't see what it is. He's trying to tell me something, but I can't pick up his message. There is interference, I'm sorry…"

"That's fine" I said. "Don't worry."

Vicki proceeded to tell me that *The Sentinella* would become huge. She made a wide gesture with her arms as she said this.

"And I picture money" she said. "I can see a pile, a big pile. No, wait. I see two piles. The second one is bigger. You're going to be rich." I smiled. I had always wished for wealth and I was quietly confident that it would arrive some day.

"I can see a world or a globe" she continued, "It's on the corner of a book. I don't know what it is, or what it means. Do you know Keidi?"

"Well I love to write" I said. "Maybe one of my books will become a world-wide best-seller." There was something even more significant that would happen down the line which would explain the 'globe on the corner of a book' but I didn't know it right then.

When my father and I delivered the June issue, he started touching up around his neck.

"What's the matter?" I asked.

"Oh, it's my rosary" he said. "I think the link has broken again, it happens a lot. It's probably caught up in my clothes."

My Dad had worn that rosary since a young man. It was the only possession he had of his father. The rosary meant even more as it had once been blessed by the Pope. One of the links was a little delicate and now and again it would break. In the past it had broken around fifty times, but miraculously my father always found it trapped down his T-shirt or caught around his belt. This time it seemed to have disappeared for good.

"No, I can't see it anywhere" said my Dad. "It must have fallen off in one of the places we delivered magazines to." He seemed upset. I tried to stay positive.

"Don't worry, I'm sure it will turn up" I said, but it didn't. Later that day my parents retraced our steps on the entire delivery run to try and find the rosary, but it was nowhere to be seen. Then my medium reading suddenly dawned on me. My grandfather wanted to pass on a message to me. Vicki was touching her neck, she couldn't pick up the message, but it was about the rosary.

"Granddad must have wanted his rosary back" I told my Dad. "I'm sure he wears it himself in heaven now."

Dad had never believed in mediums or spirits, but I got the inkling that this swayed his mind. Perhaps it happened to show that there is some truth in spirits and the other side, and help him realise that his father is still there in some form.

Negative Spell

The magazine was growing bigger and better. For the June issue I started printing seven thousand copies, and thanks to Gavin's help finding a new printer, I could afford to print them for the same cost as the previous print-run. More magazines meant more readers and more readers meant more advertisers. *The Sentinella* was hungry for success and I knew it would eat more adverts each month, becoming fatter and fatter. My profits began to increase and a huge pile of money was forming, just as Vicki the medium had predicted.

It gave me an incredible sense of power to see my bank balance creeping up and I loved the thrill of being able to afford to buy my friends lunch, or treat my parents to dinner. It made me feel like somebody, rather than just anybody. Perhaps the money was going to my head a bit. I started calculating the profits I sought to make in the future. They were high but I wanted to set a target, as I knew goal setting was imperative to achieving.

While one area of my life was flowing along nicely, others weren't. Living by myself meant I often felt lonely and depressed, and my friendship front still wasn't flourishing. All the men I thought I stood a chance with had slowly crept away and there were no new ones arriving to replace them. Hope was replaced by anguish. What made it even worse was that Zoe revealed how she had seen Rob in a bar with another girl.

"He was drooling all over her" said Zoe, clearly enjoying sharing the information with me. "Plus she was dead pretty."

Although it had only ever reached as far as my dreams, the loss of this love really affected me. I began to feel life was unfair and that I never wound up with the men I really wanted. My negative attitude towards men had existed since my teens, when I suffered from acne and was only ever laughed at by boys, while my friends dated with confidence. Any teenage crush I had was no-go and I knew it. This perception had travelled with me into adulthood, and I just couldn't shake it off. At the time I didn't know that a simple shift in thinking could bring me exactly what I wanted, including the man of my dreams. Some of June and most of July were spent feeling sorry for myself, interrupted by occasional periods on the beach topping-up my tan.

Along with the man and friend problems, I experienced an awful cockroach morning, which was a living nightmare. Every year in Torre del Mar a brigade of men, who look like they belong in Ghostbusters, descend on the town armed with deadly sprays. They aim the stuff on to treetops and bushes throughout the whole area. The spray is actually cockroach killer and for the next hour or so the hard-backed mini beasts land on the ground, writhing around desperately, in an attempt to stay alive for another sorry few minutes. By mid-morning, when shoppers come out of their shells (so to speak), the ground is literally covered with the evil looking insects. By this stage most are dead and on their backs, however, some super sized ones can still be spotted trying to make a getaway. Owners of Spanish businesses all across Torre do their best to sweep up the dead cockroaches (a task I do not envy them). As a hater of anything that crawls (apart from babies), I was horrified to be slap bang in the middle of this cockroach hell.

I was fed up with trawling the streets coming face to face with business owners and cockroaches, so I placed an advert in the July issue looking for Spanish speaking sales people to sell advertising space for *The Sentinella* on a commission only basis. I worked out I could pay someone twenty per cent of the cost of each advert sold and still make sufficient profit. Even though I was now a high-flier on the sales front, I hated it. Employing a sales person meant I could concentrate on improving the magazine's content and design, while they stomped the streets selling and creating awareness. A lady called me within the first week of the advert appearing.

"Hiya is that Keidi?" she asked with a gentle voice.

"Yes, speaking" I answered. "How can I help?"

"My name's Rachel Toller. I've seen your advert looking for sales people and I'd like to meet one day to discuss it. I speak Spanish well and I think I could give this a good go."

Her attitude convinced me to arrange a meeting for the next day. I wanted someone to start immediately.

"Hello, nice to meet you" said a pretty, red-haired lady, as she approached the bar where we had arranged to meet.

First impressions counted for a lot and this lady was confident and friendly with a warm, open face. There was something about her that I trusted explicitly and I could see she would be a hit with the advertisers. Having met a lot of people within the last ten months, I knew she had something that others do not.

"I love *The Sentinella*" she told me. "You're doing such a great job with it. You must find it hard though, doing all that work by yourself."

Her comment led me to explain the sales position in greater depth. She was intelligent and professional, as well as warm and friendly. Rachel agreed to start in July, selling adverts for the August issue.

In the meantime I performed a final spate of cold call sales. As I paraded up and down the beach front of Torrox Costa early one evening, I noticed a restaurant that I hadn't seen before, with the menus displayed in both Spanish and English. A beacon flashed in my head, so I sauntered into the empty eatery, trying my hardest to appear confident. A twenty-something Spanish lad, with wet hair and tanned skin clanked bottles behind the bar.

"Hola" I said in a louder than usual voice, so he acknowledged my presence.

"Hola" he repeated looking up from his bottle moving operation, tracing his eyes over my body from head to toe.

I explained about *The Sentinella* magazine in my best Spanish, opening the most recent issue and pushing it his way. He flicked through and looked impressed, telling me he was interested in advertising and would I like a drink. I looked deeper into his face. He looked about my age, maybe a few years older, with cheeky eyes and slightly chubby cheeks. He was handsome in a compromising way, but was his hair wet, or was that grease? It didn't appear to be drying. He looked like he had rubbed his head in a chip pan.

He introduced himself as Miguel and told me he was the boss of the restaurant and that he drove a red BMW. He clearly thought it was important to mention the car. After a long while chatting I realised that this conversation wasn't on the right track. After all, I had called in to sell an advert, not pick up a waiter. Before leaving he asked if I fancied a drink one night. I didn't fancy Miguel one stitch, but I thought he might have some fit friends. I liked the idea of going out with a Spanish man, as I would be able to practise and improve my language skills, so a week later I met Miguel for a drink.

I peered deeper into his hair. Was that grease dripping down his face? His mop was so shiny I could see my reflection in it. 'Saves having to use my mirror,' I thought. At the end of the evening, Miguel lunged his grease-drenched head towards mine, seeking a kiss. I turned my head away just in time and uttered the word "no" a number of times, so he would realise how adamant I was. He hurried off and I drove home chuckling at the bizarre night and cringing at the assumed state of Miguel's pillow.

At the same time, I also attracted a Spanish man that worked at the local internet café. I didn't yet have the internet installed at home, so checked my e-mails there every other day. The man behind the till always seemed happy to see me, but I never took too much notice until I logged into my e-mail account and noticed an e-mail from him. He was sitting right there as I opened it and read:

"Hello, I think you are very beautiful. I watch you when you come here and I would like for us to go for a coffee together some time. Please let me know when we could meet. Kisses. Jose, Cybercafe, El Morche"

I glanced up to see him tapping away at his keyboard. Maybe he had forgotten even sending me an e-mail. His eyes were deep, his hair was scruffy and flopped over his eyes in places. His features were well defined and his clothes told me he was a casual guy. I found his e-mail a little intrusive, especially knowing he had 'stolen' my e-mail address by logging on to *Hotmail* after I had left the internet café. There was one more thing bugging me. I was sure I had seen his wife and baby just a few days before. I replied saying that I didn't want coffee with him and that maybe he should think about his family.

I felt like the universe was working against me, presenting me with difficult challenges and men I didn't fancy or couldn't have. OK, so I had a good job which many people would kill for. That was the only reason I remained in Spain.

Finding employment is the biggest single factor, which forces ex-pats to return to the UK kicking and screaming. Not everyone is as lucky as me, to land such a fantastic opportunity, at no cost, but I still didn't feel particularly happy. What's the point of having a good job and earning a heap of money if there are hardly any friends, a tragic social life and no lover to compliment it? I knew I was partly to blame. I was so intent on success that I channelled all my energies into making *The Sentinella* bigger, disregarding the other areas of my life. The situation into which I had waded, caused me to experience an aggressive spell.

I had never been a big drinker before, usually only having a glass or two of spirits on a night out. However, at this time, I found myself downing vast amounts of alcohol. One night I lost my friends after a small row about nothing and fell asleep on a park bench, awoken in the morning by the sound of cars on their way to work. I knew something had to change. My behaviour was irrational and haphazard. I didn't feel like I knew myself any more All I knew was that I had moved to Spain for "a new and fantastic life" and my dream wasn't working out exactly as planned.

At this time my ex-boyfriend from the UK, Lee, and I were e-mailing each other. I felt so down in the dumps that I needed contact with someone who knew me, and it was a way of clasping hold of part of my old life in the UK. I remembered what Lee and I once had, and wondered if we had chosen to walk away from our only chance of happiness. I doubted the negativities in my mind when we were together. I forgot all our petty arguments and small issues, which would grow to larger ones down the line. Our e-mails were flirty and fun, just like the time before we originally got together. I invited him to come and see me, as I was lonely and needed the company. He accepted straight-away and by the next morning he had already booked a flight, staying for five days. I pencilled it into my diary, counting down the days until company would arrive.

It had been a long time. More than a year had passed since we had last seen each other. I thought about all the men I had met within that time. There had been a fair few; Russ, Bloody Nick, Gavin and Rob. Lee was more compatible to me than all of them put together. Well, apart from Rob anyway; the one who now drooled over his gorgeous girlfriend.

With all the money I was earning and nothing else to spend it on, I took my parents out for lunch or dinner at least once a week. It gave me one day a week off cooking, and I felt that my parents deserved a few treats, after the nine months of hell I put them through while waiting to move to El Morche. During our meals together, we started to observe the eating trends in Spanish eateries.

Lunch falls between two and five o'clock when the shops shut for *siesta*, but you can forget sandwich, crisps, yoghurt and an apple. The Spanish tuck in to a three-course meal, complete with olives, bread, wine and the rest. The restaurants are packed solid with families and workers ordering *menu del día* (menu of the day).

A typical menu costs around six or seven Euros per person, including starter, main course and dessert, as well as free bread and drink. Apparently it is Spanish law that all restaurants must serve *menu del día*. Typical starters aren't prawn cocktails or melon, but usually salad, soup or *migas* (fried bread crumbs).

Main courses frequently involve fish in some way, especially on the coast where fish is plentiful. Inland many of the main courses involve rabbit or pork for the same reasons. Unfortunately the meals, especially *menu del dias*, can prove a little plain and tedious. They are almost always served with *patatas fritas* (chips) and *ensalada* (salad). Vegetables, such as carrots, cabbage and broccoli very seldom appear on plates. For desserts, I prefer the English selection, as I have found the choice pretty bleak here. They usually offer tiramisu, *helado* (ice cream), *arroz con leche* (rice pudding) or *natillas* (custard). The latter two options are always served cold. In fact if you dare to suggest heating them up, the waiter will probably display a look of uncertainty. Custard is normally served with a rich-tea type biscuit perched on top.

Breakfast (*desayuno*) in Spain is usually crispy bread with olive oil and a thin spreading of chopped tomatoes, washed down with a *café con leche* (coffee with milk). *Churros* (long pastries) are the other obvious breakfast choice, usually dipped in sugar or thick chocolate sauce.

Coffee here is complicated as there are various ways to order it. *Café solo* is without milk and usually comes very strong and served in a glass. There are names for all different strengths of coffee, including *sombra*, which means 'shady' and is the weakest going. Next up is *nube* (cloudy) followed by the normal *café con leche* and then *mitad* (half).

Come eleven or twelve o'clock, the Spanish usually indulge in a snack, commonly a sandwich or baguette with fillings including tuna, *chorizo* (spicy sausage) or ham and cheese (*mixto*). Mid afternoon the Spanish snack on a *merienda*, maybe a slice of toast and jam, or a cake.

Then at dinner time when the Spanish have finished their working day (after 8pm) they feast on another meal, similar to that of lunch, but usually not so large.

In summer, the *heladerias* (ice cream parlours) are packed out from around 10pm until the wee hours. The choice of flavours is vast and they usually serve tasty drinks as well, including *batidos* (milkshakes) and *leche merengada* (milk and meringue, sprinkled with cinnamon).

The food in Spain is varied, but it takes some getting used to for us *guiris* (foreigners). It was fun trying out the different restaurants in Torre to see which proved the best value for money, but I soon realised I was sick of Spanish meals. I missed traditional Sunday roasts, Banoffee Pie, Carrot Cake and shopping in Asda. Overall I preferred my life in Spain to that in the UK, but now and again things arose that I missed like crazy.

Love Rekindled?

As my ex boyfriend's visit drew nearer, our e-mails grew more flirtatious. At the airport I paced up and down nervously, waiting for him to walk through the gates. Our eyes met at exactly the same time. We exchanged "hellos" and began the journey to El Morche. It was weird having him sitting next to me again after all this time. We had shared so many good times and to welcome him back into my life, even just as a friend, felt strange.

"You're looking good" he said as I drove. "Really good."

"Thanks" I said "I feel good too, living here in the sun. I love it!"

I didn't feel this was the right time to mention the negative parts of life in Spain.

Not much had changed in Lee's life. He still had the same job, the same stuck-in-a rut outlook on life and even the same shoes. Also, he still watched the same American TV shows that I despised with a passion. Two days into Lee's visit, I remembered how much he understood me, in a world where not many people do. I knew I shouldn't let that slip away, so we decided to give it another go.

"You should never have moved to Spain without my approval" Lee said later. "We should have talked it through more and waited until I was ready too."

Things with Lee and I were great. We held hands, kissed, enjoyed intimate moments and chatted loads. One evening we shared a heavy conversation about the future.

"You seem so confident now" said Lee, sipping a beer. "Before you were always insecure and needy. It's done you good moving out here, I can see that."

"Thanks" I said, glad at the positive observation. "Running the magazine has helped my confidence grow. I deal with all sorts of people now."

"Good for you" said Lee, shifting uncomfortably on his chair. "But, I'm not sure what I could do out here." He paused. "For work I mean."

"Oh, I see" I said, surprised that he was thinking about moving to Spain already. "Well I'm sure you would find something. There are lots of designer jobs advertised in the papers you know? I see them all the time."

"Yeah, but I can't speak Spanish."

"No, no…I mean jobs for English companies. You'd be surprised at how many English publications there are here.

"Hmmmmm" said Lee, thinking. "But I do really like my job in the UK. How would you feel about me moving here anyway?"

"Great" I said, with not an ounce of enthusiasm present in my voice. I wasn't expecting him to reach such a decision after five days. "It would be wonderful."

"You don't sound too convincing. There's no passion in your voice. I want you to beg me to move here with you. Not just say, 'Yeah, it'd be wonderful.'"

Lee always picked up on my thoughts.

"Sometimes you want just a little too much" I said. "If I don't display enough passion in my voice then I'm sorry, but I can't pretend to be someone I'm not."

If the truth be known, I was terrified of Lee moving here. I couldn't stomach the thought of having to share my success with someone who had taken a back seat all his life and never tried for anything. Why should he share my fruits? He waltzes over here to see me, realises how well I am doing and wants a piece of it? Is that true love?

I was questioning his feelings for me, when really I wasn't wholly sure about mine for him. I swept the thoughts to the back of my mind and continued enjoying his company until he left the next day. At the airport he hugged me and with a tear rolling down his cheek, said goodbye. I felt nothing but numbness. It was always such a roller-coaster with him and too many bends in the track ends up making one feel sick. Nonetheless, Lee and I exchanged e-mails every day. He told me he was missing me and would like to come and visit again, so we could discuss 'the way forward'. I wondered if things were really that bad in the UK.

A few weeks later he arrived once more. The numb feeling returned, stronger this time. His second visit, in stark contrast to the first, was pretty tragic. We had at least four major arguments and three out the six nights we even slept in separate beds. Despite the difficulties, we continued with the relationship. I felt like I was banging my head against a brick wall. I didn't know what he wanted from me. Did he want me to say, "Hey don't worry about a job, you can work on *The Sentinella* with me"? Did he think it would work for us to share an apartment, a life and a job so suddenly? I sure didn't. Doubts thrived in my head like an out of control ivy. In the pit of my stomach I had a really bad feeling that he just wanted a slice of my success. I had felt it before and it was escalating. They say to trust your instincts, but it's easier to say that from the outside looking in. There were feelings involved, the prospect of love and let's face it, marriage. Would I throw all that away just because of my doubts, which could be uncalled for?

Fortunately, not long after Lee left, my good friend Emma came to stay for two weeks. I was so glad to speak to her about Lee and what I should do for the best. Emma was half English, half Iranian and had an enviable skin colour and beautiful dark features, including long jet black hair. Emma, Nicole and I did everything together in the UK; rather like a female version of the three musketeers. Emma was also having boyfriend problems. She had been going out with the same man since university and felt stuck in a rut with him. He wanted them to buy a house together and she wanted fun and adventure.

"Split up with him" I said. "You're too young to settle down. Have a bit of fun, that's what life's all about."

One evening Emma and I ventured to the Virgin del Carmen fiesta in Torre del Mar, as I wanted her to see a true Spanish-style celebration. This annual event takes place on beaches across the entire coastline and for the Torre del Mar version dozens of fishing boats take to the sea to travel between the towns of Almayate and Caleta de Velez. Fishermen along the coast know the Virgin del Carmen as their patron saint. The statue of Virgin del Carmen is not only paraded through the streets, but also taken aboard a flower-adorned boat, accompanied by an array of fishing vessels. Brass bands play, crowds cheer and fireworks fill the late dusk sky.

No sooner had Emma left for the UK, than my sister called with a question.

"How would you like to be a bridesmaid?" she asked.

"What? You're getting married at long last?"

"Yeah. We thought it was about time, now that we have Charli as well. I want us all to share the same surname. It will be too confusing when she starts school otherwise."

"The thing is" I said. "I'm not sure I can be your bridesmaid. Thanks for asking, but I hate the idea of standing in front of everyone in a church."

"A church? What makes you think we're getting married in a church? A botanical gardens actually, in Gibraltar. We have it all planned you know! We're hiring out three villas for the week so everyone can stay with us before the big day and for a few days after too. And don't worry about standing in front of a lot of people, as we're only inviting twenty-five close friends and family."

I could hardly refuse being bridesmaid at my own sister's wedding.

"OK" I said. "But make sure you choose a nice dress for me."

"Oh, I've already decided that too. Your's is going to be gold, the same colour as Charli's."

I wondered whether maybe the time would come when I was arranging my wedding day. Like most girls, tying the knot was a dream.

The September 2005 issue marked *The Sentinella's* first Birthday. I couldn't believe a year had flown past since the first issue. I chuckled at the memory of having to staple all the pages together. Now the magazine had reached sixty pages, with sixteen colour pages in the middle. For the front cover I found a picture of a fairy cake with one candle and placed it on a pink background with balloons. My focus had steered away from earning enough money to live, to making the magazine as big as possible. It had grown from an initial circulation of fifteen hundred to six thousand magazines per month, which was an impressive feat in just twelve months.

Aside from the business success, my personal life wasn't rolling along so smoothly. I returned to the UK to spend another week with Lee. I figured that as he had come to me twice, it was my turn to go there. He hadn't long bought a flat and was clearly excited to show me. Problem is, I had been there, done that, about five years ago. I tried to display some pretence at excitement for his sake.

"I was thinking" said Lee randomly one day.

"Go on" I said, knowing that whenever Lee started a sentence with such words it was going to be something ridiculous.

"Well, you know I haven't long bought this flat and if I sold it now I would actually lose money on it? So I thought of a plan. You could take someone on to run *The Sentinella* for you, come back over here and get a job so we can both pay off my mortgage as soon as possible, then in a few years we would be able to sell the flat and move to Spain. What do you think?"

I laughed. Alarm bells were ringing and loudly.

"You've got to be joking?" My heart was beating hard. "There's no way that will happen. I've worked hard to get that magazine where it is. I'm not prepared for some stranger to run it. Anyway I hate it here, so I couldn't possibly live here again, working for somebody else. Your idea totally sucks."

Needless to say, we split up and I left his flat that evening to stay with a friend. That was it, game over. Now I needed to accept defeat and get on with life, with the hope of meeting a new and compatible man in the future.

Friends R Us

I'm starting a meeting group and I'd like to place an advert in your magazine" said a middle-aged sounding lady.

"That's a good idea" I replied down the phone. "It's really hard meeting good friends here...and men of course!"

I was single again and that meant I was back on the shelf, a hidden shelf come to that. I hardly ventured out much these days, maybe once a week. Hardly a brimming social life. My diary was packed with work arrangements and meetings, but no dates or nights out.

"Well" said Linda, the lady sitting in front of me wearing baggy clothes and a huge smile.

"I don't want to give people the idea that this is a dating agency, although I do hope a few relationships will flourish as a result. If I label it a dating agency it could put people off. It's more a chance to meet friends than anything else."

"Right" I said. "Sounds like you have it well thought out. "Have you thought of a name?"

"*Friends R Us*" she said, looking into my eyes searchingly for a reaction.

"Excellent" I said, putting her mind at rest. "Great name."

We discussed the advert credentials. I made a note of all the text she wanted and asked her to e-mail me the logo. I agreed to run an editorial too and promised to attend her first event. Two weeks later she called.

"Can you make the first *Friends R Us* night?" she asked. "It's on the fifteenth of September at eight pm in the *Crabtree Restaurant* in Nerja. There's a young man called Tom coming, who seems like a really nice chap. He's a real looker and he's single."

"Really? How old is he?"

"Twenty-eight" said Linda. "So about your age. Do you think you can make it along? He doesn't want to be the only one under thirty, and if you can gather anybody else to come too, then great. The more the merrier!"

I invited my writer friend, Anna, who was always game for new experiences and outings.

"Thanks for coming" said Linda, greeting Anna and I at the door. "Let me make you some name badges. Tom hasn't arrived yet, but he promised he would come. A lovely chap he is, you'll see. Now go and fetch a glass of champers from the bar. Run along."

As we chatted I noticed that we were by far the youngest people present. The rest, as suspected, were all part of the purple-rinse club. Then a light appeared. A young short guy with scruffy dark hair and a toned body strolled over to us.

"You must be Tom" said Anna confidently, leaning forward to exchange the introductory kisses.

"Yes that is I" said Tom laughing. "I was summoned over here to say hello."

"And I'm Keidi" I said. "Nice to meet you."

"Ah, so you're the girl who does that little mag? Linda told me all about you." I cringed at the thought.

"Yes, that's me. I'm to blame for all those crude jokes every month."

"Well actually, I must confess, I haven't seen a copy yet. I only arrived two weeks ago."

"Here," I said handing him a screwed up copy from my bag. "Have this one."

An OAP who advertised with me interrupted.

"Hey girl" he said. "I have some money for you here, for my last advert. I wasn't sure about the white text on a black background, but apart from that it all looked good."

Anna and Tom broke away, while I was stuck talking to Mr Boring about his boring advert selling boring mini diggers. I felt like telling him to get a life. We were at a social gathering. In my mind that didn't involve talking about publicity. As I looked at Mr Boring's thinning white hair, piggy eyes and wrinkled complexion, I could hear Anna bursting into fits of laughter from across the room. I was saved by the voice of Linda.

"Come on, it's time for everyone to sit down. Keidi, you're on that table over there, with Anna and Tom." Tom sat directly opposite me, which didn't enthral, as I was a messy eater, usually ending up with morsels stuck around my mouth and splatters adorning my top.

Nevertheless the three of us had a real laugh as we talked about our lives and what we liked and disliked about Spain. Tom worked as a builder and general odd-job man, anything going it seemed in order to earn some cash. His story wasn't uncommon here in Spain where permanent jobs were hard to come by. The next morning I awoke with a heavy head. I hadn't been on such an enjoyable night out for so long. My mobile phone sounded unexpectedly. It was Linda and she didn't waste her time with hellos and how are yous.

"So what did you think of Tom?"

"Yeah, he seemed nice. It's hard to know exactly, having only met him once, but all in all not bad."

"Well he called me just now. He wants your phone number. Is it OK for me to give it to him?"

"By all means," I said

"Oh goodie" said Linda. "You two could be the first couple I manage to get together."

Tom sent me a text later that day. 'Hi. Would you like to meet for a drink one night? Tom'. I responded a few hours later, as I wanted to play it cool. 'OK How about Thursday night?'

We met in Torrox and went for a meal, then a drink. I felt really nervous as this was like a proper date and I hadn't been on one for an age. I had forgotten what to do. I pulled on jeans and a half smart, half sexy top, with sling back shoes and a matching handbag. The chatter flowed for the whole evening and by the end of it I reached the conclusion that Tom was a down to earth guy, with a kind heart. During our date he asked a number of what seemed like pre-rehearsed questions. I imagined a tick box chart in his head, which he marked according to my answers. At the end of the night I wondered how many points I had accumulated. Had I said what he wanted to hear?

"Would you say you're a stressy person?"

"At times" I said. "My work is very stressful and when there are tight deadlines to meet, then yes, I'm stressy, but outside of work I'm pretty normal really. I like to relax when I can. How about you?"

"Me? I'm a natural born stress head."

Later we kissed. I didn't feel the Earth move. It was OK, but nothing special. I got the impression he was a bit of a control freak. Even his kiss had a certain structure.

The following morning the *Friends R Us* clan were walking in the countryside and Tom asked if I wanted to join them.

"No, I don't like walking too much" I said. "Plus I have a magazine to write, so sorry, not this time. Have fun chatting up all those wrinklies though!"

One day as I was sifting thorough my Inbox I noticed an e-mail from a guy called Keith, who had entered the magazine quiz. I noticed he had signed off with a company name. I thanked him for his answers and asking why he didn't advertise his company in *The Sentinella*. What followed was a lengthy e-mail conversation, which led me to learn that, like me, he lived in El Morche. He was twenty years old and his Dad was about to get married. Plus, he had seen me before in a shop and he fancied me. He also wrote that he owned three houses and three cars, but I didn't believe that part. I think it's just because he wanted to meet me, but he said he wanted to advertise his business in *The Sentinella*. When I saw him I was pleasantly surprised. He was tall and slender, with blonde hair and blue eyes. I didn't think 'man' when I saw him, as he still possessed that 'lost boy' look. We stayed out until late. I told him more about the magazine and he told me all about his three houses and three cars. I wondered why he felt the need to lie. Maybe because I was a successful business lady and he was a twenty year old with a lack of prospects. It was like *Catch 22*, as he was trying to impress me, but his lies had the reverse effect. The only word which bounced around my head was 'loser.' I took his mobile number at the end of the night. I thought if nothing else he would do as a drinking partner.

I had seen a lot more of Tom from *Friends R Us* too. We always kissed at the end of the night, but it never went further. I always put the barriers up and sent him home.

The Sentinella was going great and cash was pouring in. I had started meeting more people and things were looking up in most directions of my life, but I still felt unhappy and I started having mild anxiety attacks. I would be standing talking to a client and my whole body would stiffen up, I would break into a sweat and feel the need to get away as quickly as possible. I had no idea why at the time. Looking back, it was either caused by stress, or because many of my clients used me as a counsellor, off-loading their problems. They would confide in me and tell me all their lows. Other people's issues were swimming around my head, banging into the sides and causing it to hurt. I didn't mind listening if it meant I was helping and sometimes I would even offer advice, but I wasn't qualified as a counsellor, only as a journalist. I was just an ordinary girl, doing an ordinary job, yet taking on the world. What about my own problems? Who was there to listen to mine? Often I felt like running away from it all to the middle of nowhere and hiding from everyone and everything. No more people, no more *The Sentinella*, no more work.

A night out was on the cards - after all, my Birthday was looming - so I started planning one, inviting as many people as I possibly knew (not many).

Meanwhile, a new bar had just opened in Torre del Mar and the owner invited me to the launch night where there was free food and drinks for all. Turning up was a huge mistake, as I knew almost everyone in there and around half of them currently had adverts in *The Sentinella*. Work-related questions flew at me from all angles of the bar.

"Can you change the word building to construction on my advert please?"

"How's the new design coming on?"

"Can I upgrade to half page colour? How much would that be?"

"Any chance of a discount now that I've been advertising with you for six months?"

"Keidi, I saw another plumber advert in your magazine. Why? I was first in."

After 30 minutes I felt like sticking my head down the toilet and flushing it. A well-built man with a tanned face and a round head bowled over to save me. He looked like a living Malteser.

"So you're *The Sentinella* girl" he said. "Can we 'ave a word?"

He signalled to go outside, where there weren't many people. His voice sure didn't match his appearance. His accent was so South London, it hurt.

"What can I do you for?" I said.

"Sorry to talk about this on your night out mate" he said. "But, I 'ave a minibus company and I'd like to stick an ad' in your mag. What's a colour page gonna cost me? Say a good price and I might even take you up on it."

There was something about this guy that reminded me of Del-boy from *Only Fools and Horses*. The word *Fools* jumped out at me more than the *Horses*. I told him the price, more than the real price of course. I knew his game.

"You can go lower than that for me" he said. "Come on, I know you can."

"You tight arse!" I joked. "OK, just for you and as long as you swear to keep it a secret, I can do it for twenty Euros less. But that's my limit."

I knew how to play his sort. I had become an expert over the last 12 months.

"Go on then. You've twisted my arm." Now it was my time to quiz him.

"So this mini bus company you own, how much would it cost to hire one for the night to Benalmádena and back?"

"Depends. How many people? How long for?"

"There'll be around eight of us" I said, totting up people in my head. It's my Birthday in a couple of weeks and I fancy a night on the town. Say a good price and I might even take you up on it." Two could play his game.

"Oi, cheeky!" he said. "I'll have a think about it and get back to you."

"OK" I said. "But seriously now, if you offer me a really good price then I can write a free editorial about your business in the next issue."

"Cool" he said. "I'll call you, OK? I'd best go now mate, got a party to go to."

'Prick,' I thought, as he trotted off.

Party Time!

F*riends R Us* Tom and I went out a few days before my Birthday for a meal and drinks. He gave me a card.

"You may as well open it now" he said. "No need to wait till the day."

The envelope was red, like that of a Valentine's Day Card. As I tore it and saw the Birthday card lying inside I wanted the ground to open and swallow me whole. It was covered in pink and red hearts of all different shapes and sizes. I didn't know what to say.

"Thank you. That's really lovely."

Inside I was cringing. 'Had this boy fallen in love with me already? Was the heart smothered card his way of telling me so?' I sure hoped not, as the feeling certainly wasn't mutual.

The mini-bus man called with a price for hiring him and his vehicle for my Birthday night in Benalmádena. I agreed to write him a free editorial in *The Sentinella*, alongside a paying advert. I rounded up seven random people to join me, mostly men. There was Tom, Sarah and Keith, plus a few extras, who I hardly knew. Everyone met at my place, where spritzers flowed left right and centre. Traces of awkwardness flew through the air when Tom arrived. I didn't know how to act with him. I got the sense he thought we were boyfriend and girlfriend, but in my mind we were just two lonely souls who snogged sometimes. In hindsight perhaps we should have had a chat about our relationship status to clear the air between us and find out what we both thought, but it was too late for that. Keith had arrived. I sat on the sofa, with Keith next to me, stroking my leg. Tom stood on the other side of the room, near Sarah. I could see him eyeing Keith and I suspiciously. He was clearly confused, but there was nothing I could do, as things were just happening. It was out of my control. A beeping noise sounded from outside. The mini bus was waiting.

"What kind of music do you lot want to listen to?" asked mini bus man. "I've got R and B, house, techno, funk…?"

"I'll decide as I'm Birthday girl" I said. "R and B. My favourite." Keith popped open a bottle of champagne and filled a cup for me.

"Get that down you, darling" he whispered in my ear. "Oh…and Happy Birthday."

He was the only one he had congratulated me and that was only because I had reminded everyone five seconds ago. In the mini-bus Keith and I laughed and joked together. Tom looked miserable, downing champagne and brandy at an incredible rate. I thought about his heart doused Birthday card and felt a twang of guilt. 'What was I doing?' The only one who had bought me a Birthday card and I was dribbling over another man. By the time we reached Benalmádena port, where the night-life is heaving every weekend, my head was already dancing. It was just my body that needed to catch up.

"Have a good time folks" said mini bus man, as he parked. "I'll join you all later for one if that's OK?"

"Yeah by all means" I said. "Laters."

As Keith and I walked along attached by the hand, I noticed party-goers everywhere. The area was heaving with young dynamic energy, eager to have as much fun as possible. For the first time in ages I felt in my twenties again. We entered a trendy cocktail bar and I selected an orange and red concoction with a spiral straw and a paper parrot perched on top. Keith didn't dare leave my side, standing with his arm around my shoulders, watching any other males like a hawk. Then the first kiss occurred. Keith directed my head towards his and teased my lips. The champagne and cocktail had reacted with my senses, so it felt good. Out the corner of my eye I could see Tom's shocked face. After what seemed like eternity Keith detached his lips from mine and wandered off.

"I won't be long" he whispered in my ear.

Tom immediately came to speak to me.

"What's going on?" he asked. "Why did you have your tongue down Keith's throat? He's just using you, anyone can see that, anyway what happened to us?"

I reacted with surprise.

"Us? I didn't know there was an us. I know we went out a few times and kissed once or twice, but that was all. It hardly meant we were in a full blown relationship. I mean, I never saw you as my boyfriend."

The orange and red cocktail helped me say exactly what I thought. There was to be no beating around the bush tonight.

"Well super" said Tom. "Thanks a lot." He stormed off to where Sarah, Chris and Danny were talking on the other side of the bar. Keith bounded back from wherever he had been for the last five minutes.

"Everything OK?" he asked. "He wasn't giving you grief was he?" He glanced at Tom as he spoke.

"Not at all. It's nothing I can't handle, don't worry."

"Well let me know if he causes you any problems" said Keith. "I'll soon sort him out for you, the fucking little twat." His comment didn't strike me as very nice!

As the night progressed and I downed more cocktails, I grew sick to death of looking at Keith. I wanted fresh men to dance with, as that was what going out for my birthday was all about. Keith was behaving more like my shadow than a human being. Everywhere I went he stuck to my side like super-glue and I was having trouble losing him. When I finally escaped, Sarah spoke to me.

"Keidi, you really need to do something about Keith. I can't see that he's your sort. Stay away from him if I were you. You'll regret it in the morning otherwise."

The rest of my night was spent dancing in between groups so Keith wouldn't find me. Later, mini bus man turned up as promised.

"Some good moves you've got there, Keidi" he said, ogling me strutting my stuff on the dance floor.

"I know" I said, as I wound towards the dance floor then up again, swaying my hips.

Home bound I fell asleep on Keith's arm. He didn't seem at all fazed that I had hidden from him for the latter part of the night.

Next day, I didn't get up until the early afternoon. My mouth felt like the bottom of a gerbil's cage and my hair and skin stunk of alcohol. I felt disgusting and remembered why I would avoid too many nights of this nature in the UK. They were all fun and games at the time, but the aftermath was sheer hell. Nonetheless, the night helped me say "adiós" to a whole load of built-up anxiety and tension that had been festering in my head. I now felt light again and ready to tackle clients, advert designs and payment collections; all the ingredients of *The Sentinella* magazine, which in essence was my life.

I received a text from mini bus man. "*I'd love to see more of your sexy moves. Fancy a drink one night?*" I chose not to answer his message, as I had plenty of other man action to attend to. Later, when it came to paying for his advert, mini bus man caused huge problems.

"I'm not meant to be paying for it" he said down the phone. "We did a deal. You said you would give me the advert for free."

"No I didn't" I said. "I said I would write you a free editorial, that's all."

"Well that's not how I understood it," said mini bus man. "I'm sorry but I'm not paying for it and that's final."

I knew half the reason was because I hadn't accepted his invitation for a drink. I was with my parents at the time of the call, and an intense argument followed. When we had finished I was sweating like a pig, my heart was hammering, and my hands and legs were shaky.

"I hate that man" I said with a jittery voice. "And I hate doing the magazine. I've had enough." I felt like I was having a nervous breakdown.

"Why, what happened?" asked my parents. I burst into tears on the spot and couldn't stop bawling for a good fifteen minutes.

"I just feel like it's all got too much for me" I said in between sniffles. I can't deal with it any more"

The next *Friends R Us* event was held at a spacious English bar in Torrox, with a sit-down meal and a live band. Tom had met a new love interest at the events called Kate. Tom and Kate were a perfect match, they even looked alike. Kate was ten years older than he. Her personality was 'fiery' and she made no attempt to hide how desperately she wanted a baby. They were glued by the hip all night long at *La Noche de San Juan* (the night of St Juan). This is celebrated every year in Spain and it's the only night of the year on which people are legally allowed to camp on the beach. Fires are lit and barbecues prepared. At midnight the custom is to run into the sea.

A huge Guy Fawkes-like figure (which they call a doll) is burnt on the bonfire and fireworks are let off. The whole beach is brought to life and the occasion is a great excuse for a good old drunken knees up. I went to a popular beach in Nerja, called Burriana, with Sarah, Tom, Kate, Anna, and a few others. The beach is a pretty, sheltered area ideal for water sports during the day and drinking during the night. In true old-fashioned style the men went to collect firewood while us girls cooked the barbecue and prepared a side salad. Our little show seemed pretty unimpressive compared to many of the surrounding groups, who had pitched huge tents, with mini fridges, beer barrels, stereo systems and the lot. Midnight was marked by the first of the fireworks and we all ran into the sea laughing and screaming. *La Noche de San Juan* is the equivalent of summer solstice and swimming in the sea is meant to rid oneself of negative energies. It is the done thing to make a wish for the coming year.

"Get me a life?" I said under my breath, as I swept cold sea water over my body. My head was buzzing and my hair still dripping on the return leg to El Morche.

"Oh my God, the *Guardia* are over there pulling people over" said Sarah. "How much have you had to drink?"

The *Guardia Civil* is the Police force of Spain. There are two lots, the Local Police, who help school children cross the road and the like, and the scary *Guardia* who wear intimidating uniforms and carry guns and batons.

"I've had a few," I stuttered. "Probably more than I should have."

The *Guardia* sure weren't stupid. It was the night of San Juan so it was obvious that most drivers would be over the limit. They were clearly hungry to boost their statistics at the local *Comisaria* (police station). I gulped as a stern looking officer waved to pull us over. How irresponsible of me to drink more than the limit and then get behind the wheel. At that moment I really regretted my actions. If they threw me in a cell I would deserve it, but I hoped it wouldn't come to that. I was female, so I had the advantage of using my charm and innocence. The policeman handed me a black gadget, wrapped in plastic. My hands were shaking so much, I couldn't open it. Sarah helped. I had never been breathalysed before so had no idea what I was meant to do. I had seen clips in films, but I had never taken too much notice, now my time had come. I hoped Mr Guardia Civil man was in a good mood, as I placed the plastic tube in my mouth and sucked hard.

"No, no, no," said the officer, removing it from between my lips. "*Sopla, sopla.*"

"You have to blow, not suck," said Sarah, demonstrating in the air. I tried again, but nothing happened.

The policeman was becoming vexed. "*más fuerte*" he bellowed impatiently. He wanted me to blow harder. I tried a number of times, but I didn't have enough puff. I thought back to various parties I had been to in the past.

"Could you blow up some balloons," someone would ask.

"Sorry," I would utter. "I can't." Now I realised that to blow into a breathalyser was the same trick.

"*Lo siento*" I said to the policeman. "*No puedo*"

He sighed and went to speak to another officer. I was totally petrified about what might happen next. He re-approached and waved his hands in my face, mumbling something I didn't understand. My guilty complex told me to leave the car, so I opened the door.

"No, no, no," said the officer waving his hand about his face. "*Vete.*"

"He's telling us to go," said Sarah. "Come on."

"Adios," I called as we pulled away.

"Woah, that was a close one," said Sarah. "I can't believe they let you go. You'd never get away with that in England."

I smiled. If there was a God, tonight he was on my side.

Expansion

The mini bus man incident, coupled with other problematic clients, led me to consider selling the magazine. A few days later I changed my mind again. 'I'm stronger than this,' I thought. 'I can either let the bad clients effect me, or I can rise above them and show everyone what I'm made of.'

I chose the latter option and considered launching a new magazine, past Nerja on the Costa Tropical, the coastline of Granada. The Costa Tropical spanned from La Herradura to Motril and beyond, encompassing towns such as Almuñecar and Salobreña, which had a growing population of ex-pats. I was becoming increasingly frustrated with all the copycat magazines launching left, right and centre. A new one had popped up in Nerja and I wanted to add a string to my bow before they did. I began planning my strategy and launch date and decided to really accelerate my ideas in the New Year, once Christmas was out the way.

I couldn't believe that another Christmas was almost upon us. Christmas in Spain was so-so, and I missed the last minute shopping expeditions in Bromley High Street. The stores playing festive tunes, lights twinkling, children queuing to receive gifts from Santa Claus, carol singers emptying their voices to the entire town and the smell of roasted chestnuts. In Spain, Christmas just wasn't the same.

Unfortunately, it was necessary to spend the season of goodwill in Spain again as I couldn't spare even a few days for a trip back to the UK. There was too much work to do and it wasn't going to do itself. By now I had taken advert sales queen Rachel on part-time, paying her a salary rather than solely commissions. I widened her role from just selling adverts, to collecting payments and taking down advert changes. There was no way I could continue doing everything, especially with my plans to launch another magazine. When the season of goodwill was well and truly wrapped up, it was time to plan my new *The Sentinella* magazine, in the Costa Tropical.

I decided to keep it exactly the same size, style and format, as that recipe worked. I spent one day driving around each of the three main areas, La Herradura, Almuñecar and Salobreña. It took me about thirty minutes to reach the first part of the Costa Tropical, La Herradura (horseshoe, so-called because the bay is shaped like one). I noticed how scenic this stretch of the coast is, with breath-taking coves, cliffs and bays right the way along.

There were already one or two English language publications circulating in the Costa Tropical, but nothing like *The Sentinella*. I scooped up the competition for advertiser details and phone numbers. I also went into practically every English bar in the vicinity. They all had notice boards inside, covered with business cards and leaflets from English companies and individuals. I scribbled a note of their contact details to call them regarding the new magazine launch. Each day I spent an hour or so typing the contact details I had collected on to my computer. For once in my life I was being organised.

Around this time, as fate had arranged, I met a lady called Jane, an exercise junkie, who taught Yoga at a local gym. She had long dyed hair and looked a bit like Davina

McCall. She wasn't my type of person socially, but I sensed she would make an ideal sales representative for the Costa Tropical magazine. I was collecting a payment from a restaurant when I met her. She bounded up to me.

"Hey there…Keidi? I hear you're the lady who does *The Sentinella*. I love that magazine you know? It's my favourite. Leaves all the others standing by a long shot. I'm Jane by the way, nice to meet you."

I felt swamped in her personality, but let her continue.

"A friend told me you're looking for a sales person to help set up *The Sentinella* along the coast? Is that right?"

"Well yes," I said. "But…

"Brilliant. It's just that I'm looking for a part time job. I have a son you know, plus I'm going through a marriage breakdown. It'd be really good for me to get out there and sell some adverts. I'll have them all signing up straight away! I can speak Spanish fluently too, which should help."

"Give me your phone number and I'll call you," I said.

I couldn't wait around any longer, as I had more payments to collect before everywhere closed for *siesta*. It sounds like most people's idea of heaven; driving along the coast of Spain, calling in on businesses and taking their money, but it wasn't a 'feel good' job. It didn't give me a sense of well-being or purpose. In fact, I felt like all the business owners saw me as some kind of pest. At the time it didn't cross my mind that they were paying me for a service, helping them attract new customers.

The first time I waded through my Costa Tropical contacts list, I achieved great results. I dialled the first number.

"Hi. My name's Keidi and I run a magazine in the Axarquia area called *The Sentinella*. There's a new *The Sentinella* launching in your area, to cover the Costa

Tropical, and I was wondering if you might be interested in advertising in it?"

"Uhmmm, maybe" said the man on the other end.

"Well, how about we arrange a time and date to meet so I can show you the magazine and we can discuss the options?"

"OK, that sounds good" said the man.

I used this approach with the first 15 companies on my list and by the end of the afternoon I had pencilled ten meetings into my diary and made notes of who to call back. Statistically I knew I was on to a winner and that by the time I had finished, all the meetings would result in adverts.

There was one man on my list called Dave, a mountaineer, who I had trouble arranging a meeting with. He lived in Lanjarón, a small tourist village forty minutes inland from Salobreña and he kept telling me to call back when I was in that area so we could meet. Sometimes his phone wasn't within range, other times it just rang and rang, and one time he was bed-bound with flu. Finally, after a few weeks of trying, we arranged to meet at Salobreña beach.

"By the large rock" Dave said.

When I arrived, I saw the back of a man who I assumed to be Dave. He had a toned mountain climber like body and tousled brown hair. He was wearing casual clothes too, just as I had expected.

"Dave?" I asked, approaching him with a certain caution.

"Yes" he said. "Nice to meet you, let's go for a drink."

I liked the front of him, just as much as the back. He had a manly face and the most piercing blue eyes I had ever seen, which penetrated through my entire body. They were such a contrast to my plain brown ones and I couldn't stop staring into them. We talked a lot and I could see that Dave was interested in my life. At times I felt like he was undressing me with his eyes, but perhaps that's just because I wanted him to be. As I sipped cold white wine I found myself darting sly looks towards his right hand to see if he wore a wedding ring. I knew he was relatively old. I guessed around thirty-eight. Most men were married at his age, so I was surprised at the lack of ring.

"So what kind of advert do you want?" I asked. "I reckon half a page colour would be right for your business." I hesitated "Actually I'm not quite sure. What is it you do again? I know it involves mountains." Dave laughed.

"I give people on holiday in Spain guided mountain walks" he said. "Most people would get lost climbing mountains on their own, but I know the area like the back of my hand."

"Sounds cool" I said. "Well, I still think you should go for half a page colour. Do you agree?" He probably saw right through the fact that I had a half page colour with nothing on it; half a page that needed filling.

"OK" he said. "I'll take out a three month deal with you and we'll see how it goes."

"Excellent. Nice doing business with you."

"Fancy another drink?" he said, signalling towards my empty wineglass.

"Sorry, but I have to shoot off to another appointment. "It would have been nice though."

"Oh" he said. I traced disappointment in his voice. "Can I pay you in a couple of weeks? We could meet again and I'll give you cash?" There was a sense of urgency in his words, as if he wanted to meet again more than anything. I smiled.

"That would be perfect. See you soon." I could feel myself glowing with sheer horniness. Dave had managed to turn me on just by talking to me. I wondered what he could do in the bedroom.

The first issue of the Costa Tropical magazine was coming along nicely, but I needed the help of a Spanish speaking sales person, so I called Jane. I braced myself for a lengthy phone call.

"Hi Jane, it's Keidi here from The *Sentinella*."

"Hiiiiii," she answered with enthusiasm. "It's soooo good to hear from you. How are you?" I started to answer, but she disregarded the question and moved on.

"So what can I do you for? Called to ask me to work for you?"

This lady was beginning to get on my tits. There wasn't time to answer any of her questions before another turned up. My voice rose a few decibels.

"Yes," I managed to spurt out. "The Costa Tropical magazine."

I think she got the hint that I wanted her to shut up for a moment. "The first issue comes out on the first of April and I need help summoning up more adverts."

"Excellent" she said. "I knew you'd come around. Great timing as I'm desperate to earn some more cash. What's the salary by the way?" This lady sure didn't pussyfoot around.

"Well I'll pay you by the day" I said. "How about fifty Euros? You won't need to drive, as I can pick you up each morning on the way through?"

"OK" she said. "Sounds reasonable. When do I start? God, I'm really excited about this."

"Tomorrow. I'll pick you up at nine."

"OK," she said. "I'll be waiting and thanks for this, Keidi, I won't let you down, I promise."

At the same time, I had the February issue of *The Sentinella* Axarquia to put to bed. The month of February had me thinking of Valentine's Day. I always seemed to remember this day even though I never had a man to share it with. I felt down in the dumps so wrote a negative editorial in the February 2006 issue, reflecting this. I remembered when I was twelve and received my first ever Valentine's gift from my first ever boyfriend. He spent his entire three pounds, fifty pence pocket money on a teddy bear with a heart on its stomach, a chocolate shaped cupid (which I ate on the school bus home) and a cute card.

The Sentinella, February 2006
"I realised that as the years had progressed my Valentine's gifts had mysteriously depleted. If I did receive a gift from a 'casual' boyfriend rather than flowers or bears there was always some hidden agenda behind the gift. Like the time I received some chocolate body paint from a guy who I had spent just one night at the flicks with. I wasn't going to waste good chocolate though, so I ate it at home alone with a spoon, while watching Bridget Jones' Diary for the twenty-eighth time."

My sullen mood seemed to reflect throughout Torre del Mar as I noticed that a few of the English businesses, which had opened six months ago, had now closed down. Among them were a greetings card shop, a ladies fashion boutique and a luxury gift shop. Perhaps the businesses didn't work as the owners had blindly started a new profession, instead of sticking to what they know. Many people in this situation don't do their homework and this is a vital step when starting a new company. A high percentage of new businesses don't last longer than a year. If they are lucky the owners manage to sell to ignorant fellow ex-pats, while the unlucky ones simply shut down and lose their initial outlay. Not all businesses experience such poor results, but to make a venture work in Spain you have to be prepared to churn in a lot of time and effort. Unfortunately, piles of ex-pats arrive with not much sense of how things work in Spain, and falsely reckon that running a business will be a 'piece of cake.' These are usually the ones who return to the UK six months later, bankrupt. Bars tend to change hands every four or five months for the same reason.

There are always 'easy target' Brits who swoop up the opportunity to live in Spain and run a bar, but they forget to think about when they will find time for the beach and if the bar will actually take enough money to cover their bills.

I was fortunate enough to have been handed a business, free of charge, without the worry of recouping an initial outlay. All the profits that came in every month were mine, and the only outgoings I had were 'phone bills and petrol expenses. I didn't have to fork out for rent or staff costs and that was the beauty of running *The Sentinella*. At times I could see the good points, but the disadvantages shone out too.

They say in life it is important to follow your feelings; what makes you feel good and what makes you feel bad? *The Sentinella* had a hell of a lot going for it, for the right kind of person, but running it, I felt lousy and miserable. It was the payment collections that really weighed me down. I didn't feel good taking other people's hard earned cash. I tried looking at the positives rather than the negatives, in order to see me through the days, weeks and months, which rolled past. I was a successful business woman with an expanding magazine empire and it would grow even bigger in the future. That, I was sure of.

Fate

My Valentine's editorial resulted in random text messages and e-mails from single men looking for a good catch. One anonymous text read: "*Do you fancy meeting so we can use your chocolate body paint in the right way?*" Another guy sent a text asking me out for a drink. This particular chap had a reputation for asking out practically every single female he encountered. The fact he knew I was not only single but also desperate spelt an easy target. I ignored his message, instead paying particular interest to an e-mail I received. It was from the brother of a lady who had placed an advert in *The Sentinella*. She was a typical south Londoner, who I had only met a few days before, and she made a point of telling me about her photographer brother, who was moving to the area.

His name was Greg and his e-mail asked if I knew of any other photographers in the area. He said how funny he found my Valentine's editorial and that he had a similar experience with chocolate body paint in the past. He sounded rather interesting, as he freelanced for the national papers in the UK, and he had film connections. E-mails flitted back and forth for a good few weeks, until finally we arranged to meet. I didn't really know the reason for meeting, it just seemed that after so much on-line banter, it would be nice to put a name to a face.

"I'll come and find you" said Greg. "Look out for an ultra skinny man with a blue T-shirt and curly dark hair."

He didn't paint himself in particularly bright nice colours and his voice didn't match what I had imagined from the e-mails. I expected a sophisticated gentleman, but he sounded far from it. His 'ultra skinny' description had me imagining a weedy dude, like the man featured on the *Mr Muscle* adverts. Skinny men had always been a major turn off for me. I liked men with a degree of meat, as opposed to a sack of bones. A slender figure topped with a mop of brown curls approached.

"Hiya" he said. "I'm Greg. And you're Keidi, right?"

"That's it" I said. "Nice to meet you. Let's get a drink."

The meeting wasn't what I had dreamt it might be. There was no heart beating hard, fireworks in the air, or love at first sight. In fact he seemed to be avoiding eye contact. His 'ultra skinny' description was disappointingly correct. I searched for traces of muscle or manliness, but couldn't find any. The curly locks draped over his eyes needed cutting. His nose looked crooked, as if it had been broken a few times, plus he had a long scar running down his left cheekbone. Despite all this, he only looked thirty-odd, certainly not forty, which he had revealed in an earlier email. We sipped wine and spoke about our jobs. His sounded miles more interesting than mine, as he went away on tonnes of working holidays, taking photos for articles and features printed in all the nationals.

"I've just returned from Thailand" he said. "Then later I'm off to Kuala Lumpur. I'm really looking forward to it." He glanced at his watch. "The plane leaves in about six hours. It's not bad being a photographer you know. I see fantastic places all over the world."

"Lucky you" I said. "I'm stuck here collecting payments month after month. How tedious! I'm thinking of selling the magazine and jacking the whole lot in."

"Really?" asked Greg, in surprise. "Then what will you do?"

"I'll find something. Maybe write some more. That's what I really enjoy."

I got the feeling that Greg and I were meant to cross paths, maybe to illustrate the kind of life I could select if so desired.

"In the olden days I did the photo-shoots for *Happy Mondays* on tour. That was pretty intense at times," he said.

"*Happy Mondays*? You're kidding? They're one of my favourite bands. I have all their albums."

"No way! They were mad times. Usually we were off our heads." My 'sophisticated man' image flew out the window. It was replaced with 'druggy type'. The afternoon was wearing thin and Greg had a plane to catch.

"I'd better be heading home" he said. "I haven't even packed yet. I'll be back in a couple of weeks, so maybe we can catch up again then. Come round mine if you like. We could catch a film?"

"OK. Drop me a line when you're back."

I returned home deciphering Greg's personality traits one by one, creating a breakdown in my head. My conclusion was a messed up sort; a commitment phobe, who had a difficult childhood.

While delivering the magazines one month I met a man by chance while taking a coffee break. He was an elderly chap, who like many ex-pats, had moved to Spain to enjoy his retirement. He saw my pile of magazines.

"Are you the Editor of that?" he said.

"Yep, that's me."

"I knew Colin" said the man. "He did a great job with *The Sentinel*, but you've really taken it somewhere as *The Sentinella*. I bet he's shocked up there." He gestured towards the sky. "I used to work in magazines myself. Once you start, it's like an addiction, that's why I'm so interested in yours. I watch it grow every month." He paused. "Do you want to know how to make it grow even more?"

"Oooh yes please. I'm always open to suggestions."

"Well I'll tell you a secret. Play on your readership. The amount of magazines you have printed is one thing, but I put together reader surveys in the UK and did you know that for every magazine distributed, three people read it?"

"Right," I said, wondering where the conversation was heading and looking confused.

"What I'm trying to say, is that there's no reason why you can't advertise your readership figure, rather than your distribution. It would be three times as much and most people won't know the difference. Essentially you are playing on people's ignorance."

"I get you" I said, utterly impressed. "Thanks for your tip. Watch out for each new issue."

"You bet I'll be watching. And good luck, eh?"

Needless to say I added a large circle to the front page of the March issue, containing the words 'readership of 21,000'. We now had seven thousand magazines printed each month, so the statement wasn't a lie.

The first issue of *The Sentinella Tropical* Costa Tropical magazine was coming along nicely. The trips with Jane weren't particularly fruitful, but at least she was trying. She approached all the Spanish businesses, while I plagued the English ones. I was met with mixed reactions. Some signed up on the spot, others said to return when the first issue was out. All in all I made a large enough profit to make the extra effort worthwhile.

When Greg returned from Kuala Lumpur he emailed me as promised and we fixed a time for film and dinner at his place. When I saw him again it felt a little weird. This man was bordering on stranger and I was about to watch a film and eat dinner in his house; activities one might partake with an old friend or a boyfriend. His rented house was large and spacious and he had decorated it in a contemporary minimalist way. Plants stood in every room while pictures and curtains displayed smatterings of colour to brighten up the space. It felt a lot more homely than my apartment, which retained its hospital like white walls and cold marble floor.

"Make yourself at home," said Greg, heading for the kitchen. "I'm cooking spaghetti bolognaise. Do you like that?"

"It's one of my favourites," I said slumping on to the sofa and taking a magazine from the table, as if seated in a Doctor's waiting room. I heard clatterings and clankings of pots and pans, then Greg re-emerged clutching a bottle of red.

"Fancy a glass? It's nothing special, only Rioja."

"Lovely, thanks," I said, still feeling uneasy. I wasn't in my comfort zone. I was sitting in the house of a strange man having to occupy myself while he cooked dinner. Eating was difficult, as there was no proper table, just a low coffee table, which meant it was awkward for loaded fork to enter mouth without food dropping off.

"Don't worry about the mess," said Greg as a pile of spaghetti crashed to the floor.

During the film Greg and I hardly spoke, but interestingly I didn't feel uncomfortable with the silence. My mind was too glued to the film to waste my thoughts on the lack of conversation. Half-way through, he rolled a joint and puffed it slowly. The smell made me feel queasy and heavy headed.

"I think I should be heading home now," I said after the film. "Thanks so much for dinner."

"No worries. It was great to have you. Come again some time if you like? I'm away again next week though. Cambodia this time, but only for seven days."

On the drive home I decided that Greg was a lonely soul like me. It's much nicer to eat dinner and watch films with someone else, rather than on your own. He and I were in the same boat. We lived alone and didn't have many friends in the area. He was simply offering me friendship, something we both yearned for. I didn't detect any ulterior motives, I trusted him explicitly. Nevertheless, a new man distracted me from seeing Greg again…

A New Love

D ave, the fit mountain climber, e-mailed asking if I could meet him by the rock in Salobreña, to pay for his advert. I didn't know much about his life, but I knew a chemistry existed between us; a certain spark that I had never experienced before. I wore attractive clothes, which I felt confident in. I pulled on three quarter length jeans, a yellow T-shirt with a bold print design, plus matching bag and shoes.

Before my drinks appointment with a fit mountain climber, I had a number of errands to run. They all went smoothly so I arrived in Salobreña early. Feeling naughty I ate chocolate pudding drenched in chocolate sauce from a quaint café on the seafront. 'This is the life,' I thought as I shovelled spoon loads of pudding into my mouth. It tasted rich, the way I currently felt. The sun was beating down on me, warming my skin, the beach was peaceful and inviting, the café owners were friendly and happy. I imagined a fictitious interviewer quizzing me.

"So Keidi, what does your work involve?"

"Well" I would answer with a smug smile. "I drive from town to town meeting clients to collect payments. Between meetings, I stop to relax at cafes for chocolate puddings and the like. Shortly I'm meeting a fit mountain climber client, who I fancy the pants off."

My life sounded ideal. I wished I could see it like that all the time and not endure negative spells. I snapped out of my dream with the sound of the café-owner's kind voice.

"Would you like another coffee?"

"No thanks. I'd better be leaving shortly. The chocolate pudding was amazing by the way."

I wandered to the rock and saw Dave sitting outside a beach bar. He greeted me with two kisses. As our cheeks brushed I felt a surge of energy pass between us and my whole body came alive.

"Hi" he said. "Great to see you again. You're looking good."

"Thanks," I said. "You don't look 'alf bad either!"

Jesus, I came out with some really dorky things when I felt nervous! Dave laughed. He had all the attributes of a middle-aged man, including wisdom, experience and maturity; a sexy recipe for a twenty-five year old, who was sick and tired of meeting young lads more interested in getting pissed, than conversing on an intellectual level.

"So how does my advert look?"

"I upgraded you to a good page for free" I said, running my eyes over his tanned skin and firm body.

"Well in that case allow me to buy you a drink. We could share a bottle of wine."

We chatted a lot and I learnt that he was in tune with his spiritual side; a typical earthy kind, at one with nature and all that. Mountains were his life and soul. I found myself fancying him even more. He was attractive, cool and very laid back. Our body language spoke volumes, as we edged closer throughout the bottle of wine. Dave poured the last drops into my glass and his face was literally inches from my mine. Our gazes met and for a moment I felt like the Earth had stopped spinning.

"I suppose you have to rush off to another appointment now" said Dave, as I gulped the last of the wine.

"No. Actually, I don't have any more appointments today."

He smiled.

"Well in that case how about heading to the beach for a while?"

As we lay side by side, we immersed ourselves in a state of relaxation. The wine helped. We talked some more. Now the conversation was deeper and more personal.

"I'm forty-three" said Dave. "It was my Birthday yesterday. I know, I'm getting old."

His age revelation was like a slap around the face. I had considered this guy as potential boyfriend material and suddenly I discovered he was old enough to be my father. And there was more where that came from.

"I have two daughters. I was married before you see, but we've been divorced six years now."

"How old are your daughters?"

"One's twenty and the other's twenty-three."

They were almost the same age as me. Then he told me about his love of dogs, of which I had a phobia. There was one thing after another.

"I have two dogs. They're both quite big, but they're lovely and gentle. They would never hurt anybody."

So Dave was divorced with two daughters and two dogs. It should have put me off, but it didn't. I fancied him as much as before the revelations, plus I respected his honesty. For a while we didn't say a word, then he rolled his body around three-hundred and sixty degrees so we touched at the sides. He looked into my eyes and I looked into his. The Earth stopped moving again and we kissed. When we stopped we reflected on it.

"That was nice" said Dave, staring at the clouds. He turned to face me again.

"I think me and you would be good together. There's obviously something there between us. I think we can both feel it."

"Yeah definitely" I said.

"It's just my age. If you feel that's an issue then tell me." I squirmed on the sand.

"No, it's not at all. To me you're not forty-three. I don't see an age when I look at you, or talk to you. I just see Dave, the fit mountain climber." He laughed.

"Well that's OK then. You could come to see me in Lanjarón one day"

"And you can come to El Morche" I said. "We could go to the beach there. It's nicer than this one."

We walked back to my car holding hands and kissing. I felt on top of the world. My life was looking up again. So what that he was forty-three and had two daughters? Why should I let that bother me? I sensed we had been brought together for a reason, so I had to live it out. I couldn't let him slip away just because of pride, or listening to my head. This was my heart speaking and we all know hearts are more powerful than heads.

Dave had come into my life at exactly the right time. Throughout the week we kept in contact via e-mails and text messages. I invited him to stay with me at the weekend. We sunbathed on the beach, then made love. I suddenly realised why many women go for older men. A week later Dave told me he was falling in love with me. We listened to David Grey songs together and shared meaningful conversations. We were walking on air.

"How do you fancy coming to Lanjarón at the weekend?" he asked one day. "You'd love it here. Plus it's the annual water run and feria, so it's a great time to come."

"All right" I said. "But remember I'm scared of dogs."

"Oh, don't worry about them. They'll be a little friendly to begin with, but they certainly won't bite you."

The drive took an hour and a half. I crossed along the entire coast from El Morche to Salobreña, then took the motorway heading to Granada. After a long drive, the sign for Lanjarón appeared. My car chugged up mountain roads, past pouring natural springs and spinning power turbines. I gauged this wonderful sense that I would like Lanjarón. The road approaching the village was narrow and scenic. Drivers of cars heading the other away smiled as they passed and I smiled too. I passed the water factory with stacks of lorries parked outside, displaying the Lanjarón logo. Lanjarón was the largest brand name of water in southern Spain, which is said to have healing qualities. The locals could drink it for free, by simply filling their empty bottles from the natural mountain springs. I followed Dave's instructions to meet at a bar on the outskirts of town. I heard a familiar voice and approaching footsteps.

"I'm glad you got here OK" said Dave. "Bring your overnight bag and I'll drive the rest of the way. The road becomes a little difficult in places. But let's have a drink and some tapas first, eh?"

We drank wine and ate *pimientos* (peppers), *albóndigas* (meatballs) and ham croquettes. The light lunch slipped down nicely and Dave and I engaged in interesting conversation. I was delighted to be with him.

"Let's spend some time at my villa, then we can have a look around the village if you like?" I loved the way he was so decisive.

We climbed into his 4x4, which was smothered with dog hairs and generally pretty dirty. I wondered if it had ever seen a vacuum. The vehicle revved around sharp bends and up steep hills, which appeared to lead to nowhere in particular, before we arrived to some stone steps and a gate.

"This is my villa" said Dave. "Follow me."

We climbed the steps and as Dave unlatched the gate I could hear his dogs breathing and dribbling saliva. My heart beat hard.

"Down boys! Come on…get away…go inside. That's it!"

The animals strutted inside and Dave showed me around his garden, pointing out various fruit trees which he had planted himself.

"And this is the pool" he said as we descended some more steps. "I've been trying to work out how to lure the dogs in. It's so hot for them in the summer with their thick coats. The pool would really cool them down, but they seem scared of it." I was glad. I didn't want their flea ridden bodies in there with me!

"Choose a sun-lounger, while I go and pour us some drinks" said Dave. "I invented a cocktail the other day. Do you want to try it? It's my speciality."

"I'll leave it to you" I said. "Surprise me!" I wandered to the edge of Dave's terrace and admired the surrounding views. I could see the rows of power turbines whirring away like windmills and tiny cars fleeting through narrow lanes. The mountains rolled over each other and in the distance I could see the Sierra Nevada, where I had skied with Bloody Nick last year and sprained my arm.

I settled on a sun-lounger by the pool and relaxed. Dave returned with fluorescent green drinks, wearing just his swimming shorts. I had forgotten how manly his torso was. He had my favourite rugby-player build, with a wide chest span and thick upper arms. He lay on the lounger next to mine and I ran my hand across his chest. We kissed for a while, submerged in a state of bliss. Suddenly there were thudding noises. Someone was climbing the steps to his gate.

"Oh, I'll bet that's Gemma, my daughter," he said, rolling his eyes. "She's probably just being nosy, to see who my new girlfriend is."

"Is she cool with my age?" I asked, but it was too late for him to answer. Gemma was standing in front of us. I was glad I had drunk wine and mystery cocktails. I was lying on the lounger next to her father wearing nothing but a bikini. Meeting my boyfriend's daughter in this state wasn't an ideal scenario.

"Me and Juan have had a huge row," she said, wobbling. She was clearly drunk. "I don't know what to do. He's being a real arse."

I noticed Dave took care not to offer his pretty blonde daughter much advice. Instead he encouraged her to make her own decisions and learn from her mistakes. That was his philosophy and I liked it. Gemma left, apparently not at all fazed by my youthfulness.

Inside, Dave's villa was a little too well organised for my liking. The decoration was mahogany wood and dingy, and the kitchen was American-style. Colour co-ordinated cups dangled from the walls, and pots and pans hung in size order. Jars of home made concoctions stood neatly on shelves. There was chopped garlic in olive oil, chillies, root ginger and spices. Unsurprisingly, all were clearly labelled. Dog hairs clung to the sofa and floorboards, along with puddles of pet saliva. The bedroom was tidy yet haphazard, with a low bed, which almost meant sleeping on the floor. Bathroom-wise I was pretty impressed with the state-of-the-art jacuzzi tub and massage shower, which somehow didn't fit with the rest.

"So what do you think?" asked Dave.

"It's nice" I said, not sure whether that was a lie. "Very different to my apartment."

Later we wandered around Lanjarón. The streets were bustling, the atmosphere was electric and I was walking alongside a man who I admired greatly. The annual water run was due to take place that night and everyone was preparing for it. Those who chose to do so could charge along the designated 'water run' road and get wet. Those with apartments on that road took great pleasure in chucking buckets of water over their prey. Some had hose pipes, others mere water pistols. I was drenched as water ran down my T-shirt. It ran from my eyes, ears and hair and I felt like a drowned rat. The night was fantastic and completely different from anything I had ever experienced before.

After my amazing weekend it was time to focus on work again. *The Sentinella Costa Tropical* magazine was going well, but it wasn't growing any thicker. I didn't have time for both magazines and the tight deadlines for two were becoming ever more stressful, especially now I had a man in my life. I began hunting for a potential buyer. As luck would have it, I received a call from a northern couple who had just moved to Almuñecar from the UK. They wanted to place an advertisement in *The Sentinella Costa Tropical* for a cleaning business. Their names were Sue and Gary. Both were blonde and sunburnt with friendly faces and too many freckles.

"What do you think about our idea for a cleaning business?" asked Gary. "Do you think it will work?"

"Maybe" I said. "Although it's not like it's a new idea here, as there are plenty of other cleaning companies. But I'm sure there's room for more, like anything."

"We'll give it a go with a black and white page for three months then" said Gary handing me their design. "We've just moved here and we're willing to give anything a try.

We looked at a couple of franchise opportunities, but they seemed a bit boring." Neon lights flashed in my head.

"And how about you? How did you get to be running this great little magazine?" he said. They listened hard as I told them the story.

"But running two magazines is proving too much for me" I said. "I've decided to sell this one, when I find the right buyers, so if you happen to know anyone who might be interested…"

Sue and Gary looked at each other. They were clearly both thinking the same. I could read their faces like a children's picture book.

"Well we might be interested" said Gary. "Like I said, we've been looking for something like this."

I spent the next half an hour answering a wave of questions. I e-mailed them some more information later that night. The next day they were still willing and asked to see the legal contract. Another week passed and we were all sitting in my lawyer's office, ready to sign. I couldn't wait to see the back of the magazine. It was replaced by a five figure sum in my bank account. 'That was way too easy,' I thought, as I considered what car I would purchase with my earnings. The sale made me think again about Gavin's franchise idea.

"You'll make a packet" he once told me. "You'll be driving a Ferrari in no time." Material possessions weren't important to me, but money was always nice. I liked the thought of a life bathed in freedom and luxury.

I trained Sue on random days, as she was the one who would run *The Costa Tropical* magazine. I kept drumming into her the importance of trawling the streets to cold call on businesses.

"I'm not sure I will be very good at that side of it" she said.

"Well, it's very important" I stressed. "Selling adverts is how you make the profits."

As the months rolled by *The Sentinella Costa Tropical* veered downhill. Advertisers pulled out left, right and centre and eventually it was printed without any colour pages. Instead of increasing in pagination, it plummeted. Sue called to say she wanted to sell the magazine.

"Even if I can get some of our money back," she said. "At least it will be something."

I felt terrible that Gary and Sue hadn't succeeded with *The Sentinella Costa Tropical,* although I knew it wasn't my fault. I had tried my best to help them.

Bad Luck

As my relationship with Dave the mountain climber progressed I learnt more about what made him tick. I found it hard to fathom his obsession with the temperature. He recorded the morning and afternoon degrees Celsius every day onto a graph on his computer.

"Why do you that?" I asked.

"It's really so that if anyone says it's definitely colder now than it was this time last year, I can check my graph and tell them that actually they're wrong." He went on to say that last year in Lanjarón the temperature was under thirty degrees for X amount of days and over thirty degrees for Y number of days. The information darted in one ear and out the other.

"I also make a note of the wind speed" he said. After an adequate pause the conversation continued, this time broaching a different subject.

"I've made a mosquito repellent" he said, a tad too excited.

"Great!" I said, trying to sound enthusiastic.

"It's a secret recipe so I won't tell you what's in it, but it really works. I rubbed it all over me earlier. A mosquito landed on me for just a second or two then flew away. It takes a while to make though. I've had it sitting here in the sun for a week or so."

'Why don't you just go and buy some,' I thought. 'Much quicker and much less hassle.'

"It sounds really cool" I said. "You'll have to show me when I see you next." At the time I didn't realise that would mean smothering my entire body in the smelly, greasy concoction.

"Go on, rub it all over," he said as we sat around his swimming pool. "You won't get bitten, it's a proven formula. I've been testing it all week."

By the end of it I felt like I had been rolling around in an oil-rig and I sure didn't smell too hot; a cross between a mouldy garlic clove and a bottle of vinegar. Dave had some odd traits, but I put them down to his age. Maybe when I reached forty-three, I would start recording the temperature every morning and inventing strange concoctions too.

Then there was the conversation about children.

"My niece Charli is so sweet" I said. "She says all kinds of words now."

"I don't like children much" he said. The comment stunned me.

"Why not?"

"Just don't feel like I have much in common with them. It's one of the reasons I spilt up with my ex-wife. She wanted more and I didn't. They're a bit of a pain. They get in the way and cause all kinds of problems. If you want one piece of advice from me, never have any."

The conversation had drawn a line between us. From that moment, I knew our relationship wouldn't go anywhere and I began devising cunning plans to try and sway his mind.

We had arranged a trip to Cordoba the following weekend. Dave had been keeping a very close eye on the weather and revealed that the temperature had rocketed to forty-five degrees. We booked into a three star Hotel, near the Mezquitilla (mosque) for which Cordoba is famous. The heat was heavy and intense, so rather than stroll the streets in such conditions I suggested taking a horse drawn carriage around the town. The horse clip-clopped over cobbled streets and down narrow lanes, while the driver occasionally shouted the name of what we had just passed. There are a lack of gardens in Cordoba, so all the homes and restaurants consist of patio areas, strewn with plants and pretty water features. In one eatery, I counted more than 100 pot plants and I sure didn't envy whoever had the joyous task of watering them all.

The next day we checked out the famous Mezquita, a place of worship for the Moors of the eighth century. It housed beautifully carved arches, expertly designed with intricate patterns. I wondered how long it would have taken skilled craftsmen to complete such an elaborate project. Unfortunately the Mezquita was 'ruined' by Christians, who had left their mark by imposing ghastly statues and deathly images of Jesus Christ and the Virgin Mary around the entire edge. Nowadays it is completely surrounded.

Dave and I grew closer on our trip away and saying "goodbye" was a little difficult. I was used to his company and didn't want to spend time alone again.

The following weekend I stayed in by myself, as Dave was trekking the Sierra Nevada with clients, and camping in the hills. I didn't know how he could be bothered. Sleeping in a tent without the luxuries of toilets and baths would drive me mad. I used the opportunity to talk to my sister about her wedding. It was fast approaching and I was faced with the bridesmaid role. I had a long gold chiffon dress to wear and pointed gold shoes. My hair would just have to make do as it came, as it was too short to pull into any fancy style. There were twenty-five of us all staying in three large villas, in a mountain village called Almogía, thirty minutes inland from Málaga City. Tragic visions of *Big Brother* poured through my brain. I half expected we would have to 'vote off' family members according to who proved the most annoying. The villas each had their own swimming pools plus a jacuzzi to share. All the ingredients of a typical *Big Brother* house in fact. I was overjoyed that there were no chickens to feed, no food budget, and no partly obscured cameras. It was a week's holiday for all and everyone was excited.

The journey to Almogía was long and bumpy. I was surprised that my elderly car made it in one piece. I sensed it wasn't far from its death and I planned to buy a new car after the wedding. I had my eyes feasted on a black Citroen C1, with air conditioning and electric windows. It was a step up from the basic model of Ford Ka which I had driven for the last seven years. Now I felt like I deserved something a little more luxurious.

My parents, my brother, his girlfriend and I all stayed in the same villa, while the groom's family stayed in another, and friends of my sister in the remaining. The wedding day and overnight stay in Gibraltar came around quickly and before I knew it, we were all donning our wedding clothes, and sipping champagne before the ceremony. Charli looked adorable and my sister, Kami, looked radiant. I looked attractive too in the long dress, which I thought would make my thin body look drowned. To reach the groom and guests, Kami and I had to descend a number of steps. I was dead nervous as we made our way towards them. We took our positions at the foot of the steps and the vows were exchanged. Tears lingered in everyone's eyes as the bride and groom kissed at the end, then there was a huge cheer. It had only taken ten years, but finally they were married!

A stretch limousine took them back to Almogía, where a local Spanish restaurant hosted a sit down meal. The rest of us made our way in our own vehicles, adorned with white ribbons strategically tied around aerials and door handles. The done thing in Spain when newly-weds drive to the reception, is for wedding guests to hoot their car horns when passing through towns and villages, so we contributed to the tradition.

The reception went down well. The Spanish restaurant put on a great show, providing as much beer, wine and soft drink as we could possibly sink, plus a three-course meal. Speeches followed and the traditional cutting of the cake. Back at the villa, the pool had been scattered with rose petals and 'Just Married' banners hung above the door frames. We sat around the pool, while the more adventurous jumped in. More drinks were passed around and as night fell we hit the disco, where the men played pool and the women chin wagged. The event was just like a normal wedding, except that it all took place in Spain, with guaranteed sunshine and perfect hospitality.

A few weeks later, I received a phone call from Dave. He sounded down.

"Keidi, I have some bad news. I have to go away for a while, to the French Alps. My business partner there has fallen and broken her ankle. She isn't in any state to work and she has lots of clients to take trekking. I have to take her place. She says her ankle might not be mended for six weeks or more."

"Oh" I said, stumped for words. "When do you leave?"

"In three days" he said. "I'll come to see you before I go, if that's OK?"

"That would be nice" I said before hanging up. I felt totally downtrodden.

Dave came to say "goodbye". We made love then he turned to me.

"Sorry, but I have something on my mind. I found out that my daughter's boyfriend hit her. I want to talk to her before I leave for the Alps. Tonight's the only chance I'll get, so I can't stay the night with you."

I felt sad because I knew our relationship was fading away. There were too many factors against it; the age difference, the dogs, the not wanting children, his daughters. It was doomed. Now it was just about facing the music and moving on.

Empty Heart

A s the heat was now unbearable and my Ford Ka was deteriorating daily, I decided to invest in a new car, with the essential bonus of air conditioning. I chose a black Citroen C1, which looked trendy, and was small enough to park in practically any space.

Having recently said goodbye to my boyfriend Dave, who was now trekking in the French Alps, I felt emotionally raw, but through the tears I ploughed on with *The Sentinella*. It was the magazine's second Birthday and the last year seemed to have sprouted wings and flown by. I made a big deal out of the front page and hired a photographer. I bought party poppers, confetti, cake, champagne, balloons, bubbles, a birthday banner and a big red balloon shaped as the number '2'. The idea was to hold a mini-party on my parent's balcony. There was me and my parents, Rachel the sales-lady and her twelve year old daughter. We arranged the props, then gathered around a table for the photo shoot.

"Come on and get some bubbly down you," said the photographer, as he snapped his camera into position. "We want to see you having fun and enjoying yourself."

After, we celebrated with cake. Within two years the magazine had grown from forty pages to an impressive one hundred and twelve. The pagination had almost tripled in twenty-four months. I was becoming known as 'the success story' and readers began following my progress, as if I was some kind of a celebrity.

Nevertheless I was becoming sick to death of running the magazine. When it was smaller I had a life alongside it, but as the pagination increased, I worked like a mad-woman. I woke at eight am, turned my computer on straight-away, then answered e-mails, sent e-mails, made calls and chased payments. The next four hours were spent visiting clients and collecting payments or taking down advert details. In the afternoon I made more 'phone calls and designed and wrote the magazine. Weekends were also spent designing and writing.

Life became rather like a treadmill, totally devoid of any fun or excitement. I began thinking about my life in the UK. There, I spent most of the day sitting at a desk writing articles and features, but at least I had the weekends free to do what I wanted. Not that I ever did much. I would usually sleep till midday then spend the rest of the day moping around and cutting my toenails. I sighed at all that wasted time, which could have been spent visiting art galleries and museums, lunching with friends, or watching shows and films. From the outside, I had the dream life, but I was still moaning.

Ex-pats emigrate all over the world in search of fresh pastures and a better life, but even though the surroundings change, often the need to make money does not, so in the end most of us find ourselves doing a similar thing, but in a different country. Moving abroad certainly wasn't the paradise I had once imagined. I was bored of seeing and speaking to the same clients month in and month out; making the same calls, sending the same e-mails, chasing the same people for payments. I needed a change and I thought again about selling the magazine.

Deep down though, I wasn't sure. 'You're on to a good thing here,' my inner voice told me. 'If you don't want to run it any more, fine, but don't sell it. You may regret it later on.'

So I continued slogging away, trusting that a brilliant brainwave would materialise when I least expected it.

With my boyfriend Dave away in the Alps, I felt lonely again too. At least before he left, I could squeeze him in once a week, which was enough to make me feel human again.

His communication was terrible. I expected him to call or text, but I didn't hear anything until a week later. He e-mailed now and again, but his messages were brief and direct and he didn't once suggest that he missed me. Anxious for reaction, I e-mailed him:

"I'm sorry Dave, but I don't feel like our relationship will ever go anywhere, so I don't see the point of continuing with it. This isn't easy for me to say, but I feel we would be better off splitting up. What do you think? Keidi x"

I cried as I typed and my hand shook as I clicked 'send'. His answer blew me away. It was a long e-mail, revealing his deep love and intense feelings for me. On the other hand he said how he couldn't see it working, largely due to the children issue. Tears flooded from my eyes as I read *"I love you Keidi"* over and over again. So there I was, twenty-five and single again. I felt like one of those unlucky-in-love types. Men didn't seem to hang around too long with me. I considered taping the next candidate to a chair.

The summer was drawing to a close and now that I was single again I wanted to milk as much joy from it as humanly possible, so Sarah and I arranged a few days away in the Costa de la Luz. This coastal region, which translates as Coast of the Light, is situated past Gibraltar to the west of Málaga airport. The journey by car takes around two and a half hours from El Morche. I had heard a lot about the area. Golden beaches, greenery (praise the Lord!) and slightly fresher weather sounded heavenly in comparison to the dirty sand, barren landscape and sweltering temperatures on the Costa del Sol. Tarifa was our first point of call, a young, trendy resort where cool surfer dudes hang out.

Finding a Hotel wasn't as easy as anticipated. All rooms were fully booked and we were desperate. Only one Hotel could offer us a room for the Sunday night.

"We might need to sleep on the beach, or in my car even," I said, feeling disappointed. "Or we could try our luck in the next town along?"

"Yeah, I reckon we should try there first," Sarah said.

I was glad. Me and tents didn't really go. I liked my creature comforts too much. I wasn't prepared to swap them for sleeping on ants nests and taking cold communal showers.

Before heading to Barbate, we explored Tarifa. The main hub was buzzing and picturesque, but the residential outskirts were shabby and run-down. Hideous apartment blocks were draped with the washing of entire families and walls ruined by bad boy Graffiti. The beach didn't impress either. I counted thirty overflowing bins from one spot. Barbate was even worse than Tarifa. We found a basic room, but it was better than nothing. I rang around more Hotels to try and book a room for the duration of our stay. I covered every coastal town from Tarifa to Chiclana, but there were no rooms anywhere. Now I knew how Mary and Joseph must have felt in Bethlehem.

"How about trying an inland village?" said Sarah, not wishing to give up so easily. Bingo! The first Hotel I called had rooms for both Friday and Saturday nights, so I booked.

The next morning things were looking up. We found a nice beach in Caños de Meca, which was plagued with hippies. This was it, the Costa de la Luz we had imagined. It was an amazing stretch painted with pure golden sand, lapped by crystal clear water and with an interesting tide-line. Five hours of sunbathing, one picnic and one horrible toilet experience later we headed to our next Hotel in a village called Vejer. The Hotel was huge and located on the main road at the foot of the village. The reception and room were immaculate. There was even a brand new swimming pool, which had only been open for two days. We had struck lucky. The previous day suddenly made sense, this was our reward. Immersed in luxury, perched on a sun bed, with drink in one hand, ice cream in the other, we could finally inhale total relaxation.

Night-time took us to Zahara de las Atunes, my favourite town of the trip. It was very quaint, just the right size and it boasted a classy restaurant on the beach front, serving exquisite dishes, such as cheese stuffed aubergines and wok fried vegetables followed by ice cream and hot raspberries. The food was to die for and the setting divine. We couldn't have hoped for better.

We spent our last day and night in Tarifa, the place everyone raves about. Our whale-watching trip was cancelled as a result of strong winds, and sitting on the beach was like being in the middle of a full blown sandstorm, so instead we opted to eat, drink and be merry. Night-time began in a steak-house, where I felt strangely drawn to the waiter, who was English with enviable Spanish language skills. He was friendly and chatty and he even gave us a glass of wine on the house.

"Where are you ladies off to tonight then?" he asked.

"We don't know the area very well" I said. "Where can you recommend?"

"Well I knock off work at one in the morning, so if you meet me here, I'll take you to the best bars if you like."

"Cool" said Sarah and I in unison.

Night time is when Tarifa comes alive. We saw the town in a whole different light, a better light, a light we didn't want to go out. Crazy characters introduced themselves in various bars and we accompanied a few of them to a night club. I was disappointed as I fancied the waiter we said we would meet, but I was too drunk to really care. Sarah spoke to the DJ and I was being chatted up by an Italian with a crooked nose and bad breath. I desperately wanted him to go away, but he stuck to me like a leech. I looked up for a second and caught a sight of Chris, the waiter from earlier, with a group of friends. I looked up again and he had vanished.

"Mind if I interrupt" said a voice to my right. Chris was standing right there. I turned to the Italian.

"Sorry" I said. "It was nice talking to you..."

He slipped away and Chris and I chatted and laughed. Our auras were so magnetised that it didn't take long for us to kiss.

"I have an idea," he said. "How do you fancy going to this really cool beach-front disco I know?"

The rest of the night was a blur. I had a great time, but I didn't see Chris as a potential boyfriend. He lived too far away and after my experience with Dave, long distance relationships sucked.

Awakening

The October issue reached an all time high of a hundred and twenty-four pages. I couldn't believe how large the magazine was growing, and clients and readers couldn't either.

"Wow! Your magazine is huge now, isn't it?" said one friendly reader. "Good on you. You work so hard that you deserve the success. Keep it up!"

We're only advertising with you from now on," said a happy client, and other comments of praise poured in from all directions. I didn't know what to say any more, I had run out of words, but it was important to refrain from acting too smug.

"Well, yeah it's doing OK I guess," I would say.

In between all the hard work, I needed another a holiday, so when my good friend Nicole suggested a long weekend in Barcelona, I couldn't refuse. Living in El Morche was like residing in a bubble, trapped inside an area which lacks atmosphere, culture, people and style. Barcelona provided all the missing ingredients, plus more. The city is nestled in the Catalan region of Spain, so the locals speak the Catalan dialect, rather than traditional Spanish. We stayed in a small Hotel on a road off of Las Ramblas, which is the main tourist-fuelled street, stretching to the marina. As we wormed along Las Ramblas, my eyes darted from person to person.

"Look at that man," I said. "He's got green hair." "The height of that lady's shoes is amazing. I would topple over for sure." "Did you see the state of that guy's clothes?"

"I see people like this all the time in London," said Nicole. "You need to get out more, girl!"

The sad fact was she was right. I had been hidden away from real life for the last two and a half years. I had forgotten about the splendour of other human beings and how amazingly fantastic and individual we all were. I had been so focused on *The Sentinella* that my social life had suffered extortionately and this trip resulted in yet more neon lights flashing in my head. 'Get a life. Get a life!'

Entertainers lined either side of Las Ramblas. Some stood stone still, human statues, painted from head to toe in gold. Others wore fairy wings, or strange costumes. One man donned a suit with pieces of fruit hanging from it. Another dressed as a baby and lay in a pram. Every time someone peered in to take a look the man burst into tears, just like a real baby. Passers-by threw their loose coins into buckets. The 'clink clink' sound was interspersed with squealing traffic, hearty laughter and the beeping of pedestrian crossings. I absorbed the whole lot, overwhelmed to have discovered variety again. They say variety is the spice of life and now I knew why. I thought about the variety offered on the Costa del Sol. "Do you want your ice cream in a cone or a pot? Agua sin or con gas?" There wasn't a whole lot!

"Ooooh, I want to go on one of those," I said, pointing at an orange tourist bus with no hat. The tourist mobile slithered through the busy streets of Barcelona.

"And the fascinating building to your right is the Manzana de la Discordia designed by Antoni Gaudí," said the commentator. "Apple of Discord is a contemporary pun playing with the word "manzana," meaning at the same time "block of houses" and "apple." A few minutes later his voice piped up again.

"And Casa Calvet to the left was designed by Antoni Gaudí for the textile manager Pere Calvet." Another five minutes passed, then:

"Gaudi's most famous work can be seen if you look to your right. The Sagrada Familia built this temple in eighteen eighty-three, but Gaudí died before he had the chance to finish it."

If I failed to learn anything else from this trip, at least I now knew that Gaudí designed most of the architecture of Barcelona.

Mornings in Barcelona were my favourite time. La Boqueria, the open-aired food market, was the perfect venue for eating breakfast. The locals congregated there for bread with olive oil and tomatoes. Everyone sat around a large square bar chatting and eating. The atmosphere was cracking. I watched the hustling and bustling housewives buying fresh fruit and vegetables and market sellers yelling their special offers in a bid to attract more customers. Nicole and I visited La Boqueria every morning for a punnet of blueberries, a bag of walnuts and a cup of strawberry and kiwi juice. Evenings were spent eating more fine food, drinking wine, paying rip-off prices selected especially for tourists, then as the night progressed choosing vodka over wine and making tits of ourselves on various dance floors.

When I returned to El Morche I felt sad, as I had grown to love the busy streets of Barcelona and the dynamic vibrancy they contained. I wished I could swap it with El Morche for a while, to restock on the hectic city life I craved. I thought of Anna, my writer friend, who had recently jetted off to Sydney, Australia, to take part in a writer's resident scheme, allowing her a free stay in a posh Hotel. Now she had the right idea. All she had to do in exchange was spend a few hours watering the flowers every day, which seemed a fair enough trade. Anna used the opportunity to complete her first fictional novel, with a spiritual twist. It was she who inspired me to gain greater interest about spirituality. Whenever we met for lunch our conversations would turn to this subject and it led me to delve deeper into the world of spirituality and that bright white light which is our higher self.

One topic I became more interested in than any other was the Karma. I sought relief from the belief that everyone's Karma today is a product of their past. When clients failed to pay me for adverts, I would think about the Karma and immediately feel better. I knew there was something in this theory and I began applying the principles of Buddhism to my own life. Real Buddhists spend a lot of their day meditating to enhance their qualities and help others through loving compassion and kindness. They also use visualisation and positive thought techniques to achieve manifestation of the things they want. The principle is more commonly known as the Law of Attraction, and teaches us how we can all act like magnets to resonate with the universe and achieve greater wealth, love, success and happiness. I had always thought along the same lines anyway, with *The Sentinella*. Every night I would flick through the magazine then think about how clients and readers would perceive this content, always in a positive way. I would lay the latest issue face up by the side of my bed and ponder it as I drifted off to sleep. This nightly routine is the main reason I believe *The Sentinella* grew so successfully.

While she was down-under, Anna and I kept in regular contact via e-mail. I was interested in her amazing opportunity and how she was using it to her advantage. I was really happy for her and the adventure she was experiencing. When she returned fourteen weeks later, I felt like I knew her better than ever.

"It's so good to see you," I said. "You're looking really happy and healthy."

"I feel it," said Anna. "The whole time in Oz was excellent. So much happened and I met some really fab people, including some nice men. One in particular…"

"Tell me all about him," I said as we ordered lunch.

"Oh and before I forget, I bought you a little gift," said Anna, handing me a flat item wrapped in a white paper bag. It was a postcard with a red border and in the centre, the Chinese symbol for Love.

"I thought you could stick it up in your apartment and focus on it," she said. "You never know, it might help you meet the man of your dreams."

As soon as I got home, I blue tacked it to my living room wall, facing north. There was something about the north, which seemed more viable than the south. Maybe all this spiritual stuff was going to my head a bit. Certain relatives who didn't understand the concept, would have said so, but at that time in my life it felt right, as though it was meant to be.

As I sat in on my own for yet another Saturday night and eyed Anna's Love Postcard gift, I reviewed how much I would like to meet a man. Not just any man, but one who would play an important part in my life.

The next day a random thought entered my head. 'You should join a dating agency, maybe something on-line; one of those websites where you can meet people.' I decided it would have to be a Spanish website, as I couldn't exactly fly back to the UK every time a man wanted to meet me. So I logged-on to the Spanish version of a popular website and chose their *encuentros* section, which means dating, I entered my personal details, added a photo and wrote a few sentences about myself in bad Spanish. I was excited at the prospect of meeting new men, but also a little dubious because of the common speculation that such websites attract perverts. As soon as I had posted my details I began receiving messages.

Men reeled in at an incredible rate. Many were clearly just after a shag, as English girls have a stereotypical 'easy' reputation. I instantly deleted messages of this nature. I 'met' five or six men that seemed really nice, but it was difficult to tell over an on-line messenger service. After 'chatting' to one particular guy for a good few weeks we finally arranged to meet in Nerja. I couldn't face one more Saturday night watching tortuous Spanish television shows!

'Could he be the one?' I wondered.

Energy Flow

My first internet date was called Ros, aged thirty-five. He lived in Granada and had a shaven head and large blue eyes, which made his face worth looking at. I hoped he would appear the same in real life, as he did on my computer screen. We both had web-cams so watched each other as we chatted on messenger. I wasn't overjoyed at the prospect of meeting. In truth, I was disappointed that I had resorted to meeting men in this way. Why wasn't I a normal twenty-something girl, who met men in bars and nightclubs? Maybe the small fact that I didn't go to bars and nightclubs had something to do with it. As I parked my car, I could see the silhouette of Ros perched on a barstool with a drink. It was odd to speak to each other in person, after so much time 'chatting' via the computer. It was much more personal this way, where there were no barriers between us. When our eyes met at that initial moment I almost keeled over with unease. I felt awkward and sensed an uncomfortable expectancy that we must fancy each other. The tense introduction dissolved and we entered into a more relaxed conversation.

"Let's go to the discos," said Ros later. "I want see you dance."

"No way," I said. "I'm happy to go to the discos, but don't expect me to dance. I'm nowhere near drunk enough for that!"

At the disco square we found a free space to stand and my entire body tensed up as I stood there like one of the human statues on Las Ramblas in Barcelona. I knew Ros wanted me to dance with him because he insisted on moving his hips flamenco-style, gyrating his crotch in rhythm to the music. I tried swaying slightly to trick my body into the mood, but it didn't want to know. My legs stiffened like planks of wood and my arms hung awkwardly by my sides. Suddenly Ros grabbed me around the waist, flinging me in all directions, compelling my body to move as he wished. He was determined I would dance with him, even if through physical force. Hating every second, I squirmed free from Ros's grasp. The loss of control I felt as he paraded me around the dance floor was not only embarrassing, but also uncalled for. I darted outside and inhaled a lungful of fresh air.

"Why you no want dance with me?" asked Ros? "I sad."

"Well I'm sad too" I said. "I'm not some kind of rag doll that you can fling around as you please. I'm a human being and if I don't want to dance, then you should respect that."

"Sorry" said Ros. "Just wanted you to have fun."

"Well I don't want to dance tonight" I said. "I'm happy just talking."

"OK" said Ros, "Let's talk more."

Later as I walked to my car, Ros asked if he could stay the night with me in my apartment.

"No way!" I said. "I don't even know you. You'll have to take a taxi home." I was deeply offended that Ros had asked such a ludicrous question, and the next day I deleted Ros from my messenger contact list and blocked incoming messages from him. I couldn't see the point continuing to 'chat', as time is precious. Looking back perhaps the instant deletion was a little cruel. An e-mail pointing out my differing expectations and asking him not to make contact again might have been a nicer way of dealing with him.

My list now contained five men, who all or all of whom seemed like semi-decent beings. One in particular intrigued me, as he often asked if we could have tea together one afternoon. He wasn't like the other men, wanting to meet in the evening and ply me with alcohol, so he could have his wicked way. Unless he planned to spike my tea, I couldn't see how he had any ulterior motives. Plus, he looked attractive in the photos and I liked the way he used a lot of smiling faces in his messages. That signalled a happy guy and we all prefer happy people than sad ones. His name was Chema and he lived in Málaga. The journey there seemed an effort so I kept putting off meeting, using my workload as the excuse. Another potential was a guy called David, a lawyer, who lived in Benalmádena. He had the habit of sitting at his computer with no shirt on, knowing the web-cam was displaying everything back to me on the other end.

"You can take your top off too if you like," he said one day. That did it. Another deletion. Men had to tread very carefully with me. It didn't take much for me to hit that delete button. It was a process of elimination and the one remaining man would be the winner.

At this time Sarah and I were getting itchy feet again and fancied a change of scenery. We booked a weekend away to Tangiers, in Morocco. Southern Spain practically touches Morocco, so trips there are cheap and the journey time brief. For two nights in a three-star star Hotel, including breakfast, ferry crossing and transfers, it cost a mere sixty-five Euros each. The ferry left from Algeciras, which is a little further along than Gibraltar, on the Costa de la Luz, the coastline after the Costa del Sol heading west from Marbella. After an hour and a half on board the ferry, we moored at Tangier port. We were in Africa! The dress code in Tangiers was very different than in Spain. Men donned long white robes and the women completely covered their skin with a tunic and multi-coloured scarves for the hair. I felt like we had landed in a different world. After the ferry ride we were hungry so the first task was to find food. On the way out of the Hotel a tour guide stopped us.

"Where you girls going?" asked a short man with grey hair.

"For lunch then to the shops" I said, taken aback by his intrusive question.

"You want shops? I take you shops" he said rubbing his hands together with glee. "Come on. I take you to good shop, biggest and best in Tangiers."

"But we are hungry now" I said growing suspicious. "We want lunch first."

"I see" said the man. He looked at his watch. "In one hour we meet here and I take you shops in car." Our legs ached and being taxied to the shops sure beat walking.

"OK" I said. "See you in one hour."

What we anticipated as a drop off amongst all the lovely shops, transpired to be an underhand phone call and a meet with a young Moroccan chap. Our chauffeur then left us to follow this stranger through narrow winding streets and back allies. Men ogled us from all angles.

"I don't like this" said Sarah looking anxious. "We have no idea where he's taking us."

"Don't worry" I said. "I think it'll be OK."

For some reason I trusted him. He led us to a huge shop that seemed to appear from the middle of nowhere. There were shelves stacked with all sorts of goodies;

silverware, jewellery, carpets, mirrors, exquisite boxes, statues, lanterns and more.

"This way ladies" said a voice.

Three men, who looked like they belonged in the Moroccan Mafia, led us through the expanse of richness, talking us through prices.

"How much is this?" asked Sarah, holding up a small tin teapot.

"Well that's a really beautiful piece" said one man. "But you're a very beautiful lady so we can offer it to you for much less than the real price. We can make you a special price, for a special lady. What's your name?"

"Sarah" she said without hesitation.

"And where are you from Sarah?"

"Well I live in Spain, but I'm originally from Croydon in the UK."

"I have a cousin there" said the man. "Yes Croydon is such a lovely place."

"Really?" said Sarah. "Whereabouts in Croydon does your cousin live?"

"Oh I forget the name of the street" he said. "Quite close to the centre."

"What a small world it is!" said Sarah, deeply enthused.

I was listening to the whole conversation, inwardly furious at their game plan. They were using the oldest trick in the book to try and win Sarah's trust. I could see right through their tactics. They were trying to make her feel special and important so that she parted with her money and bought their goods.

"So this pure silver ornament" said the man picking it up, as if it were a diamond. It sure didn't look like silver to me, just an old piece of tin, rusting in places.

"We can offer it to you for one hundred and twenty Euros. Only for you, mind." I burst into laughter.

"A hundred and twenty Euros?" I said, coughing. "I hope you're not being serious? That isn't worth anywhere near that amount. I wouldn't even pay twelve for it!" The man shot me a dangerous glance. He turned back to Sarah, ignoring my comments.

"What do you think Sarah?" She appeared to be considering the offer.

"Ummm, it seems a bit expensive" she said. "I'll think about it."

The men followed us around the shop like sheep, describing every item we so much as looked at. They were beginning to get my goat.

"Look, I'm sorry if this appears rude" I said. "But we would feel much more comfortable if you left us alone to look around. We are more likely to buy things that way."

The trio of Moroccans sighed and retreated, watching us from afar instead. It gave me the chance to speak to Sarah about the tin teapot she had fallen in love with.

"You're not really thinking about paying a hundred and twenty Euros for that thing are you?" I whispered. "It's not worth anywhere near that."

"No" she said. "I thought they might say twenty at the very most, but not a hundred and twenty."

"If you really like it, you should haggle," I said. "That's what they all do over here. It's part of their culture. They expect it."

Later Sarah offered twenty Euros for the piece, but the men refused, continuing to pressurise, trying to talk her around. Sarah wouldn't budge on her decided price. We left the shop without having made a single purchase, much to the disappointment of the shopkeepers who didn't even bother saying "goodbye". We were back amidst labyrinth streets with no return lift to the Hotel. It then hit me that the over-friendly tour guide, who dropped us off for shopping in the heart of Tangiers, clearly earned a commission from any sales. He wouldn't be happy hearing we hadn't spent a single cent.

"Well, let's explore Tangiers!" I said.

Working our way back, we passed ramshackle chicken stalls, old ladies selling fruit by the wayside, muttering beggars and perverse men. Among all this pandemonium, us two English girls felt like swans on a pond of ugly ducklings.

"You ladies want to see sights?" asked a scrawny man with yellow sticky out teeth, who looked like he hadn't seen food for weeks, not to mention a toothbrush.

"No, we're quite all right" I said. We had been warned to ignore all men, but that was easier said than done. It didn't feel right.

"Where are you going?" he probed. I tried not to answer.

"Are you going shops?" he continued. "I know good shops. Let me take you." That old nutshell.

"Look, can you just leave us alone," I said without flinching. "We want to walk around by ourselves…Please?"

He continued following us, so we fled into a shop and hid behind some rolled up carpets until he disappeared.

The shops were a real treat and we bought bags of gifts. There were elaborate lanterns, beautiful mirrors, handmade purses and plenty more. I couldn't believe my eyes and it was all so cheap.

Dining later was difficult, as we had decided upon the traditional Moroccan dish of couscous, followed by fresh mint tea, but finding a restaurant that served couscous was impossible. They catered for tourists and that was all. I thought what a shame that was. We were in Morocco, yet surrounded by western food outlets.

The following day we took an excursion into the mountains surrounding Tangiers and to see the attractions of the area. We were also taken to more shops and, God forbid, the Mafia shop, where we had spent time the day before. Sarah and I lingered in the corner, avoiding eye contact with any of the shopkeepers. It was too late.

"Seventy Euros and it's yours" said the youngest of the men, waving the tin teapot under Sarah's nose.

"No, it's still too expensive" said Sarah. "It's really lovely but I just can't afford that sort of money. I'm sorry."

"Make me an offer then," said the man.

"Twenty is all I can afford," she said. The man made a snorting sound as if to say 'no way', before moving on to his next victim.

Next we went to look around the Moroccan street market. I can't describe the scene as anything less than magical. It felt like we were in a film and I had to pinch myself to make sure I was really there. Stall holders rammed their goods under our noses as we passed, in some cases restraining us from continuing until we acknowledged them. If we expressed even a slight interest in anything, then they would spend the next thirty minutes trying to talk us round to buying it. Small children sat on the ground weaving carpets, while adults painted stones. I tried to keep my eyes focused into the distance, rather than on what was going on in front of me. We were also taken to a *herbolistería* (health food shop), where a characteristic chap talked us through the pros and cons of various natural remedies. I purchased orange blossom oil, which he described as 'good for insomnia sufferers'.

"Put two drops in a glass of water, drink it before going to bed and you'll be out like a light in no time," he said. I hadn't slept well the night before so put it to the test.

"We were in the middle of a conversation then all of a sudden you didn't answer," said Sarah the next morning. "I looked over and you were fast asleep. That orange blossom oil must really work!" It sure beat counting sheep!

When we returned to mainland Spain I couldn't stop thinking about Morocco. Everything I saw was so surreal, yet so deeply magical and I knew I would return in the future.

Work took a back seat at this time, as I had some more time out in my free week a month. This is the week when the magazines were at the printers. Usually I spent it preparing the next issue and catching up on life's necessary chores, like cleaning and bank visits, but my friend Liz from the UK, who had visited once before, announced she had booked a flight here again.

During her stay, the weather took a turn for the worse and the rain plummeted. It didn't stop from the moment she stepped off BA, to the moment she stepped on it again.

"Oh well, we may as well clear out your apartment" she said. "It's looking really cluttered you know."

"Are you sure you don't mind?" I said.

"Well there's not much else we can do," she said, peering out the window at rain clouds. We got to work clearing cupboards, dusting, throwing and polishing.

"This has to go" said Liz, chucking a furry monkey holding a heart into a large black sack.

"B-b-but…." I stammered.

"Look" she reminded me. "You're twenty-six now. Cuddly monkeys are for three-year-olds."

When the de-junk mission was accomplished we took three bulging bags to the charity shop, and binned a further three. As I glanced around my new-look, now minimalist, apartment I felt lighter, clearer, as if I was making way for changes and space, creating room for my energy to flow in new directions, on routes where it previously couldn't. I smiled. This was the beginning of something new, a new phase on my life-path. I had always believed in the power of energy flow and the concept of Feng Shui, the Chinese art of creating positive energy around the home. A plant here, a picture there, a wind-chime outside the door. Even little changes can have positive influences on our luck, well-being and good health. I told Liz about my on-line dating.

"That Chema sounds interesting" she said. "Why don't you meet him?"

She was right. The next time he asked me to meet I would accept. He had already asked about six times, so I hoped he hadn't given up.

Christmas was approaching for the third time since I had moved to Spain and I was still slogging away on *The Sentinella*. By this point I was like a zombie. First thing in the morning I would switch on my computer, check my e-mails and make phone calls, before fitting in a couple of slices of toast for breakfast. Then I would be rooted to my computer chair for the next four hours, designing adverts and inserting editorial. A quick lunch, then back to the dreaded chair for the same again in the afternoon. I wasn't logging off until eleven or twelve at night and I even worked solidly through two weekends each month. I had to, in order to crawl through the workload. One day, as I sat on the dread chair, looking at a half-finished magazine, a sudden thought entered my head. 'My sister Kami and her husband Tony could run the magazine.'

Tony had always done jobs which involved meeting customers on the road, so I had him down as the delivery man, sales person and payment collector. Kami had always worked in phone-based roles. Her latest job was on the end of a phone, taking the 999 calls for Kent Police. She fitted in nicely as the secretary and designer; calling advertisers for changes to their publicity, trying to win new clients over the phone and designing the adverts and magazine. The formula worked superbly. Why hadn't I thought of it before? Plus Kami and Tony moving to Spain would mean little Charli, my adorable two-year-old niece, living here too. I pictured our Mum's face as she heard the news. She would be over the moon to have her one and only granddaughter here at last. I called my sister that night and I didn't waste my time beating around the bush, so I put the question to her almost immediately.

"Seriously?" she asked.

"Yeah" I said. "I thought it might suit you two, and it's a much nicer environment here to bring Charli up."

"Well I'm definitely interested" she said. "I've wanted to move there for ages, but we couldn't before as we didn't have a job to come to. I'll talk to Tony tonight and we'll get back to you."

The following morning she called early.

"Tony and I spoke last night…" She paused and I held my breath. "…And we would love to move out there and run the magazine!"

There was pure joy in her voice, as if they had been waiting for such an opportunity for an age. My stomach did something weird as if a knot had just untied itself. I enjoyed a real feel-good sensation. The untied knot also represented a feeling of liberation and freedom, the opportunity for change.

My sister and brother-in-law had a lot to prepare; a house to rent out, notices to hand in, people to tell and car boot sales to organise. They planned to arrive at the beginning of February 2007, in time to work on the April issue. That meant my hard working self, motoring on for another few months. I knew I could hold out. The knowledge of them coming to take the workload off my hands somehow kept me going.

At last there was a light at the end of the tunnel and new horizons, with the prospect of excitement and change. Hallelujah to the high heavens! I knew the step made sense. I had offered my sister and her family a chance to move to Spain and take on a lucrative business. I had handed them an opportunity on a plate, as one had been handed to me two and a half years ago. Returning the favour to someone else was the very least I could do.

There comes a point in everyone's life, when it is time to step back from the task in hand and review where we are going next and whether our current role actually makes us happy. This was mine. I trusted my sister and brother in law explicitly and I knew they wouldn't let me down.

Magic In The Air

From a spiritual point of view, they say if you create a space in one part of your life, it's automatically filled with something else. The day after the deal was settled with my sister about moving to Spain and taking over *The Sentinella*, Chema asked me out again. He worked in a Hotel in Torremolinos and had been given two free tickets to a magic show.

We arranged to meet at Málaga bus station. As the bus pulled in, I scanned the people scattered outside. He had described himself as 'tall', apparently that was all I would need to identify him. I could vaguely make out a towering guy through the window. Two months of chatting on messenger and finally we were meeting in real life. My insides were on fire.

"Hello, Keidi?" said the man, with a sexy Spanish accent.

"Yes" I said, relieved that the conversation had commenced in English. I hoped it continued that way.

"I'm Chema" he said smiling. His face seemed warm and friendly; familiar even.

"I've parked nearby," he said, leading me to a silver Ford Focus. The awkwardness I felt as I climbed into the passenger seat vanished after a few minutes. In fact I felt strangely relaxed around this man. He exuded a calm, gentle aura, which I plugged into, as if I fed off his tranquil nature. This contrasted nicely with my over-active mind and busy nature.

"Fancy a tea first?" he asked. "At last!"

"Yes that sounds good" I said. "Sorry I kept putting off meeting you, but I've been so busy."

En-route to the *tetería* (tea shop) light banter chipped away at my barriers. The real Keidi was slowly emerging. I still felt on edge, but not nearly as much as I had presumed. *Teterías* are becoming a more popular concept in Spain. Málaga has five or six now, most Moroccan in style. Chema held the door open for me as we entered. I liked the fact he was a gentleman.

"Let's go upstairs" he said. "I know a nice place we can sit."

It was a medium sized room with Moroccan pouffes around the edge and handmade rugs littering the wooden floor and hanging from the walls. In the middle, low tables supported candles and incense sticks. There were no chairs, so instead customers sat on pouffes on the floor, drinking and chatting. There were groups of friends giggling, and happy couples kissing, all under the age of thirty-five. I plonked onto a free pouffe with my legs stretched out to the side. There was something liberating about sitting on the floor, it felt more intimate and less formal.

"Have you ever been to a *tetería* before?" asked Chema, perhaps noticing my overwhelmed facial expressions.

"Never" I said. "I haven't seen anything like this in London even."

"I come all the time" said Chema. "There are lots of teas to choose from." He was right. The menu was at least eight pages thick, packed with infusions, remedies, milkshakes, juices and coffees. I couldn't believe the choice. I could see the waiter approaching out of the corner of my eye so panicked and settled upon a *Hinojo* tea, as I liked the name. The waiter sniggered and said something to Chema, which I didn't understand.

"He says that tea is a remedy for people who have trouble doing poo-poos," said Chema, smiling. I couldn't help but see the funny side.

"Well that's not for me then," I said laughing. "I have no trouble with my poo-poos! I'll have a chocolate and mint tea instead."

The brew arrived in an intricately designed silver teapot, accompanied by a glass cup with colourful patterns circling the rim. Exotic music played in the background and burning incense created a heavenly subdued ambience. The whole shebang was like walking through a door to another part of the world.

"Your name is very unusual" said Chema. "I've never heard of another Keidi before."

"My parents made it up" I said. "They liked the name Heidi, but preferred names beginning with K, so changed the H to a K and came up with Keidi. I know it's a little strange, but it reflects my personality! How about you? Where does Chema come from? Why aren't you a Paco or a Miguel like all the other Spanish men?"

"Actually I'm a Jose" he said laughing. "My name is Jose Maria and most Spanish names have what we call a *nick*. The nick for Jose Maria is Chema. My friends call me Chema rather than Jose. I prefer it."

As our teapots emptied I realised I was enjoying myself. It was the first time in a while. I wasn't worrying about deadlines or advert designs, I wasn't stressing about late payments or articles. I was purely focused on speaking and listening to this kind-hearted man, who had sprung into my life, already making a difference.

"Do you fancy going for something to eat before the show?" he asked. "I know a really nice restaurant just outside Málaga."

"Yeah! I'm starving" I said.

The restaurant was almost as perfect as the *tetería*. It was set on top of a hill and the views over Málaga were incredible. The whole city was illuminated like a Christmas tree. I could even make out the headlights of individual cars worming their way throughout traffic jams. We sat next to a large window to enjoy the views throughout our meal. I ordered a pasta dish. I made sure the pasta in question wasn't long, just simple shapes. Long pasta was too difficult to eat in a lady-like manner, plus I could never get the gist of curling it around my fork to refrain from slurping up the stray bits. Some people make it look so easy, but not me. I was one of those long pasta slurpers. Dinner dates had always petrified me for this reason. I cringed at the thought of facing a prospective lover with stray food particles planted around my mouth. Fortunately a plate of spirals arrived. Just one dig of the fork was all they needed to safely enter my mouth. I was pleased with myself at the end of the meal, as everything had gone smoothly. On previous dates I had propelled food across the table, catapulted it on to walls, spilt drinks and once I even set a menu on fire.

"Now to the Magic Show!" said Chema as we settled back into his car.

"What exactly is this show all about?" I asked.

"There are three magicians working together to perform various tricks" he said. "I've heard good things about it, and I'm into magic myself. Well, I know a few tricks."

"Oooh a man of many talents" I said. "I'm intrigued."

The show was just as Chema described. A trio of magicians flung each other in the air, set each other on fire, dangled from dangerous places and levitated each other, seemingly by the power of the mind. At half-time Chema told me the secrets behind some of the tricks and even showed me a few of his own. At one point I thought he was going to kiss me. His eyes seemed to connect with mine. After the show I thought the night was over, but Chema suggested a drink at a bar in Benalmádena port.

"What would you like to drink?" he asked. I couldn't think of any alcoholic beverages for the life of me. It was late and I felt tired. I wanted him to just order anything for me so I didn't need to rack my brains.

"You should try *ron miel con limón*" he said. "It's really nice."

"What on earth is that?" I asked.

"Honey rum with lemon," said Chema slowly, considering the English translation.

"OK" I said. "Order me one of those!"

The drink was sweet and blended perfectly with the bitter lemon juice, rather like a miracle offering. We grew to know more about each other and had fun learning phrases in each other's languages. Again, all worries and concerns escaped my mind and I felt free. I was even surprising myself at how much fun I could have when I allowed. This was what life was really about, not cramming in as much work as possible into the few hours God sends each day.

"I really want to kiss you," said Chema suddenly, gazing into my eyes.

One second we had been laughing at the meaning of *años* (years) as opposed to *anos* (anus) and the way many English mix the words up, and the next a kiss had entered the equation. I was taken aback by Chema's comment and hugely embarrassed. I could feel my cheeks warming, probably turning a deep shade of red.

"No" I said. "I'm too shy."

"Would you like another drink then?"

"OK" I answered. Despite the looming kiss I didn't want the night to end.

"Now you have to kiss me" said Chema. "I got you another drink!"

With that his head appeared right in front of my face and he pressed his lips against mine. I was in a state of shock. There were people all around and I felt like crawling into my shell and hiding. A kiss occurred, but it wasn't how I anticipated. In the car we kissed again, but there was something vague and unsure about it. I was relieved when Chema pulled his head away and started the car. I had parked at the bus station in Torre del Mar, so he dropped me there.

"Thanks for bringing me back" I said. "And thanks also for tonight. I had a really nice time."

"Me too" said Chema. "Hopefully we can meet again soon." I didn't allow the opportunity for further kissing and left the car practically as soon as it had stopped.

"'Bye" I called back.

Many girls would have been overjoyed at ending the date with a kiss, but in this case not me. I felt uncomfortable and I knew I was holding back. I liked the idea of kissing a man when the time was right, not just for the sake of it. This way I could inject my heart and soul into it, rather than just an unsure surface. Driving home to El Morche thoughts of the night meandered around my mind, like moths around a light. There was the magical *tetería*, the beautiful restaurant and views, the entertaining magic show and the buzzing bar in Benalmádena. Everything had gone so perfectly, except of course for the kiss. When I got home I noticed the Love Postcard Anna had given me as a gift from Australia. I wondered if it had cast a spell over my life and found me a good man to share the golden feeling with.

Chema and I met a week later and spent a day at Fuengirola Zoo to watch the animals, and another at

Benamáldena Sea Life Centre to ogle the contents of various aquariums. We kissed again and this time, probably because I was 'ready', it stirred the birth of deeper feelings inside. Later, Chema dropped me home in El Morche. When he saw where I lived he was deeply shocked.

"I had no idea you lived so near my ex-girlfriend" he said with his lower jaw almost touching the floor.

"Why? Where does she live?" I asked as we stood in my living room.

"There," said Chema, pointing to my balcony doors. "In the house across the road, you look down on it from your balcony."

"You're joking?" I said. "That's unbelievable." What a small world it was.

The night before Christmas Eve, Chema came to my apartment so we could exchange gifts. I had wrapped up a bottle of *Ron Miel* for him and a lemon, as I knew from our night in Benalmádena that it was his favourite drink. I also bought a box of his favourite chocolates, which happened to be mine too. Chema handed me a wrapped gift.

"Happy Christmas," he said. It appeared to be a bottle shape. I cringed as I tore back the paper. I hoped the words *Ron Miel* didn't meet my eyes. How embarrassing that would be, to buy each other the same Christmas presents, but the bottle inside was *Ron Miel* and there was even a bag of lemons with it!

"Let's have a glass now," I said, trying to mask my thoughts of his exact same gift. I left it hidden in the corner, desperately trying to avoid an awkward scene.

"I have something else for you too" he said passing me another wrapped item, this one with no definite structure or shape. It felt soft and I pulled out a furry green frog with a pink and orange scarf and words on its chest reading *eres mi princesa* (you are my princess). The gift was perfect. I couldn't believe how spot on it was. I had loved frogs since the age of three when I received my first, pink with green eyes, which I unimaginatively named Pinkie. As he left that night I handed him his present.

"You can't open it until tomorrow night" I said. "When you open the rest of your gifts." I hoped the weight wouldn't give the secret away.

Every second I spent with Chema, he grew on me a little more.

"Do you fancy spending a weekend away?" he asked some time in the New Year. "Maybe in Antequera or Ronda?" Both were areas on my list of places to visit.

"That's a great idea" I said. "I'd love to. Perhaps we can fit in both."

Antequera is situated inland, about forty minutes from Málaga City and it is an area where there is plenty to see and do. The first day was chilly, but we braved the biting winds and drove to El Torcal National Park, a famous area of outstanding natural beauty, to walk one of the three signposted walks. It is a rocky spot, which offers breathtaking views over the surrounding region. We buttoned our coats as high as they would allow, avoiding the icy patches as we made our way to the 'easy' route, which was estimated to take fifty minutes. It was close to zero degrees, so the quicker the walk the better. After forty-five minutes of following signs, admiring views, taking photos, wiping runny noses and trying to keep warm, we had come full circle. It was such a luxury to clamber into the car and turn on the heating full blast. On the way back to Antequera town we stopped to admire *La Peña de los Enamorados* (Lover's Mountain), which resembles the head of an Indian lying down.

"There's a story behind this mountain" said Chema with his arm draped around my shoulders. "Years ago, two lovers who couldn't be together because of their religions, jumped together from the mountain to commit suicide."

"Oh right" I said. "That's a bit morbid."

On the second day we visited Ronda. It was another cold day, which meant constant walking in order to keep warm. The gorge area of Ronda is the most famous and visually stunning part. We looked down upon it from the old bridge. It appeared so vast and in truth a little daunting. I hoped the bridge didn't choose to collapse, as it was a hell of a long way down. At the bottom an innocent river flowed about its daily business, contrasting with the stark clay rocks of the gorge. Another wonderful viewing point was from the quaint park. I could have spent hours simply looking down upon the rolling hills, overtaking each other in their haste. 'Jack and Jill would be in their essence here,' I thought.

Changing Times

T*he Sentinella* website needed a face-lift and as I had big plans to expand *The Sentinella* in other ways, there wasn't a better time. I contacted a web designer, who had advertised with me for a while. We met over a coffee to discuss how I wanted the information presented.

In the February issue I officially launched *The Sentinella Business Opportunity*. With my sister and brother-in-law about to start running the Axarquia edition, I was now in the position to get the idea off the ground. I could provide all the help and support potential candidates needed. I had gained sufficient knowledge during the last two and a half years to start *The Sentinella* anywhere where an ex-pat community had formed.

The idea was to charge a one-off fee for people to run *The Sentinella* within a designated area and I formed a company called *The Sentinella Global Magazine Network*. I couldn't help but think big. It was just my way. I designed an advert including all the key points; no costly overheads, no need to employ staff, no need for stock, work at home with hours to suit your lifestyle, etc. In with the cost, networkers would receive necessary software and related guide books; a comprehensive training booklet; branded stationery, price lists, order forms, business cards, back issues and a USB stick containing all the documents needed, including a magazine template.

I placed Planet Earth on the front page, along with *The Sentinella Global Magazine Network* logo, which appeared as the symbol for a globe integrating the colours blue and yellow. The name of the company appeared around the edge, spanning a full circle. Now I knew what my medium had meant by 'the globe on the corner of the book'!

My idea was to start with the Network in Spain, then introduce *The Sentinella* to other countries, including the UK, France, Portugal and America, anywhere English speaking communities lived or gathered. I didn't see why if it worked in Spain, it wouldn't work anywhere else. Most people I spoke to said how brilliant the idea was. Every time I switched on the TV I saw globes. They jumped out at me everywhere I went. As I walked down the street, a globe hit me from a billboard advertisement. If I was listening to my car radio the words *el mundo* (the world) would be mentioned more than usual. It was like my guardian angel was saying, "this really is a great idea. Go for it!" I already had the basis of a contract from when I sold *The Sentinella Costa Tropical* to Sue and Gary. An hour's work and a re-wording of the key terms resulted in a new and improved version.

The February issue hadn't even come out and I already had my first client, who wanted two areas, with the plan of combining them into one magazine! He was my web designer. The very first person to read about the opportunity and he wanted to buy two areas. I saw this as a hugely positive sign. He, along with a friend who had recently closed a family-run business, bought the Benalmádena area with neighbouring Fuengirola and Mijas. I could understand why they had chosen these areas. They were not only popular tourist destinations, but also saturated with ex-pat residents. We negotiated an agreed total price, they signed their contract immediately and I had the first lump sum of cash in my hand.

As soon as the February magazine was distributed, I received more phone calls from interested parties.

"I'm enquiring about the business opportunity."

"Can you tell me the price?"

"What areas are available?"

"How much profit can I expect to make within the first month?"

"Can I buy two or three areas?"

Questions bombarded my brain, flying at me from all angles. Then a lady called.

"My son has recently moved here with his wife and they are looking to run a business together. They are interested in the Málaga area. Can you tell me exactly where that covers?"

"Certainly. Málaga City, Alhaurín el Grande, Alhaurín de la Torre, Cártama, Torremolinos and Rincón de la Victoria."

The area was a large one, but statistically I knew there weren't quite so many English people there. When I met the young couple who were taking it on I realised that if anyone could make it work there, it was them. The lady was Australian and very confident. She had all the ingredients to make a damn good sales person, and I couldn't see her letting non-paying clients slip through the net. Her husband struck me as the quiet one, but great with computers. Between them they possessed everything needed to whisk *The Sentinella Málaga* into shape. A few weeks after our first meeting and after many alterations to the original contract, they finally signed on the dotted line. Area number three signed and sealed!

The fourth area was sold to a four-some, two couples, who were good friends. One couple lived near Marbella, but knew *The Sentinella* from when they previously lived in the Axarquia area. The other couple still lived in the Axarquia region, in a mountain village, near Lake Viñuela. They signed within two days of phoning me.

Then, after the initial burst of sales, something peculiar happened, the business sales came to an abrupt halt. I sold four areas within one month then six slipped by with none. Calls and e-mails continued to flow in, but no one was biting. Plus I had lost focus, largely due to the magazine handover.

My sister Kami and her husband Tony had arrived in Spain and they wanted to make a start on *The Sentinella* as soon as possible. They took a few weeks to settle in and found a perfect three-bed ground-floor apartment to rent on Baviera Golf Course complex near Torre del Mar.

The hand over process went smoothly. Kami picked up the design and production role quickly and Tony became the new face of *The Sentinella*, delivering the magazines, visiting clients for advert changes, collecting payments and seeking new business leads. Between them, all the work was wrapped up each month. My small role involved writing the editorial and I could have the whole lot done within a day. At first I found it hard to let go of the magazine and I kept my phone number printed inside, constantly speaking to my sister to make sure everything was in hand, but as the months rolled by I managed to detach myself.

I began planning a much-needed holiday with Chema. Our relationship was still thriving and my last proper holiday was some four years ago. Running the magazine meant that it was difficult, often impossible, to plan a holiday. Within my time in Spain I had taken the odd trip back to the UK (always in the dregs of winter) and spent a couple of weekends away in Barcelona, Antequera,

Morocco and the like, but no real biggy. After careful consideration we opted for America. We decided to really make a meal of it and spend three weeks there. The first part of the holiday would be spent in Orlando then we planned to drive to New York, stopping at places of interest along the way. The idea was to leave the hire car in New York, fly back to Orlando and spend the last ten days park hopping in Disney World.

America was absolutely heaven-sent wonderful! Chema and I had an amazing time and during the three weeks we didn't argue once. I was a little worried before leaving, as they say time away on holiday can make or break a relationship. It sure made ours. After ten days of constant fun and excitement, the dreaded return flight loomed.

"I don't want to go home" I said, the day before we were due to leave.

"Me neither" he said. "I love it here."

We had enjoyed such a wonderful experience together, one which we would never forget.

I had been worried at how Kami and Tony would cope without me, but everything had run smoothly. There were a few phone calls to make and e-mails to send, but the whole magazine had been designed, with just a few holes to fill with articles.

With work and relationship my life was perfect, but I still didn't have a great deal of friends. Sarah and Anna were my only decent ones and fortunately they were real gems. Anna called me not long after America.

"How do you fancy coming to visit a Buddhist Retreat Centre with me this weekend?" she said. "I'm writing the final chapter of my book and I need to visit it to round things off."

"I'd love to come," I said. "I'm really interested in Buddhism. We can make a day of it if you like?"

We set off early one Sunday to the Alpujarras, the mountain range where the Sierra Nevada ski resort is located. The Alpujarras are made up of an array of tiny villages including three more famous, set in the Poqueira Gorge. We stopped in Pampaneira for a spot of lunch. There was a cute plaza with three main restaurant choices surrounded by various shops and stalls selling hand-crafted items, as well as the typical fare of the region. An interesting looking chap with a straggly beard and a fold-up chair plonked himself in the centre of all the action to entertain diners with his accordion. Every now and then, usually when someone had dropped coins in his upturned hat, he would couple the music with singing. His unique character added something to the already heaving atmosphere in Pampaneira. We ordered *Patatas a lo Pobre* (poor man's potatoes), a typical dish of the area containing peppers, potatoes, omelette and a perhaps too generous serving of olive oil.

"Right now let's go and find this Buddhist Centre" I said with a full stomach.

O Sel Ling (place of clear light) was founded in 1982 by a Tibetan Monk, on land donated by the local villages. The turn off to the centre was nothing more than a narrow dirt track, rocky and uneven in places.

"I don't think my car's too happy" I said as it moaned and groaned over large rocks, making whooshing sounds with its wheels.

"You're right" said Anna. "Let's park and walk the rest of the way."

"Walk?" I said. "All the way up there?" I pointed far to the top of the mountain where there was a glimpse of colour flapping in the wind, which Anna guessed was a string of Tibetan prayer flags.

"Yeah" said Anna. "Come on, we've got all afternoon, and it'll be nice to have some exercise. It looks further than it actually is, I'm sure."

I hoped she was right as we began the ascent by foot, with the hot afternoon sun pounding upon our heads. The Tibetan prayer flags slowly became closer, tempting us to reach them with their whispers.

"Finally" said Anna, as we arrived at the foot of a *Stupa*, which is a holy object filled with prayers, mantras, texts and relics of higher beings. The Buddhist custom is to walk around the *Stupa* in a clockwise direction. This is said to create a positive energy, purifying any negative thoughts immediately. We followed the path further to another holy object, where there was the chance to make an offering to Buddha. Some people had left coins or jewellery; others small dolls or key rings. I rummaged in my bag and could find nothing but a green paper-clip, so left that. Wind chimes sang with the breeze. I interpreted their sounds as answers to our hopes and prayers. The next stop was the prayer room. We removed our shoes before entering, following the instructions of a sign on the door. Inside I could literally feel the energy of the silence pounding through my brain. Within the centre's grounds there was also a library full of spiritual-related books. A wise elderly Spanish lady brewed some herbal teas and told us more about the centre. We left feeling invigorated and purified, an amazing feeling which I can not describe sufficiently in words.

"Thanks so much for inviting me" I said. "I feel so calm and refreshed after that."

"Yeah me too" said Anna. "And I think I can finish my final chapter now."

I was glad. Anna and I were both aspiring authors and writing books at the same time. I wished her the same amount of luck and success as I wished upon myself.

With my recent insight into manifestation and creating the dream life via visualisation and meditation techniques, I created a notice-board full of images of the things I wanted in my life. There were illustrations of some children's book characters I had developed, a one dollar bill with the figure '1,000,000' penned on it, my *Sentinella Network* training booklet and a map of the world. Now I just had to sit back and await the results which would create the next chapter in my life...

Where I Am Now

Dear Lord/Buddha/Higher Being,
Thank you for answering all my prayers and
helping me to feel happy in Spain.
Long may it continue…
Amen

Five action-packed years down the line from moving to Spain, this is the point to describe where I am now.

I still live alone in my one-bed apartment in El Morche, a stone's throw from the wonderfully sandy beach, where I spend time watching the sea, catching rays, writing, reading and thinking.

Rewinding five and a half years I cringe at the knowledge that I wasted so many days perched on smelly trains, surrounded by lifeless commuters on their way to another day of hell at the office. I shiver at the thought of sitting on the same swivel chair day in and out, working for a company I never understood the purpose of, for a boss who spent most his days peering into the bottom of a pint glass and shagging secretaries in five-star hotel rooms. I freeze at the thought of all those bygone days, which I'm glad are safely stored in the past with the lid tightly shut, hopefully never to be released or repeated.

Life really is what you make it. Yes, I received a certain degree of luck to help me reach where I am today, but then that luck wouldn't have happened had I chosen to continue with the daily treadmill, which so many people simply grin and bear.

Having met whole array of men over the last three years, I am now the happiest that I have ever been in a relationship. Chema is kind-hearted, gentle, calm, funny, loving and my pillar of strength. Since meeting him my Spanish has improved ten-fold and I crave fluency in the future (when I am not too shy to practice).

Meeting fellow English peeps here has been easy. On the other hand, meeting good friends with whom I share common interests is a different kettle of fish. Fortunately I now have a couple of good chums, who have helped me through the long days and nights. But on the whole, the ex-pat community is of a certain breed. Engaging in mindless gossip seems to be the preferred pastime; either that or getting swept into drunken brawls.

The Sentinella continues to succeed. Since I took it over, it has rocketed from an original forty pages, to an average of one hundred and twenty-four pages a month. Now that my sister and brother-in-law run the Axarquia issue, I plan to expand *The Sentinella* more via the franchising concept when the time is right.

Generally I feel at a completely different place right now. Instead of running around like a headless chicken I have time and space, creating relaxation and calm. I love researching spirituality and related topics via the internet, reading books and of course, writing. My second book, The Path, is almost complete. It's a fiction book focusing on the themes of life after death and our mission on Earth, both topics which I am very passionate about.

Five years ago, I was staying in my parent's apartment with just them and my clothes as my life. Now, in 2009, I run a successful business, am planning to move in with my boyfriend and look forward to developing my writing career.

I sigh as I rekindle the memories of the events and experiences which paved the way to my current situation. Everything is flowing so smoothly and at last I am living the life I anticipated when I first announced to friends and rellies, "I'm moving to Spain."

Business Guidelines

How to start, run and expand a business in Spain
by Keidi Keating, Director of *The Sentinella Global Magazine Network*

1. Do your homework.

This is essential to ensure the business you have in mind is likely to work in the area planned. For example, if you are planning to open an English bar in Valencia, scout the region for other English bars. How many are there? Do they all appear to be doing well? How do the busier ones stand out from the rest? How do their prices compare? Is there a large enough English community to warrant the opening of yet another English bar? Perhaps pay a visit to the local *Ayuntamiento* (Town Hall) to check out ex-pat population figures.

That is just he beginning. Then, of course, you need to identify a prime location for your bar, sort out suppliers, bar staff and all the rest.

2. Budget realistically.

Many business starters fail to put enough money aside to cover all the costs they are likely to encounter. Remember that unexpected expenses will probably crop up. Do not make the mistake of running out of cash before you have even opened or set up your business. Of course, you can always take out a loan, but then there are the interest payments to consider.

3. Be sensible.

Will your overheads, such as rent, cover what the business is likely to take? For example, if you plan to open a greetings card shop, selling cards at €2.50 each with a €1.50 mark-up and your rent is €600 a month, you will need to sell 400 cards a month (that's 100 a week, or 20 a day) just to break even. And remember rent won't be your only outgoing if running a shop.

4. Spread the word.

Talk to as many people as possible about your new venture – friends, acquaintances, even people you meet for the first time. Word of mouth is a great starting point to get your business talked about and believe me the ex-pat community in Spain likes to gossip!

5. Advertise.

Yes, here's where *The Sentinella* comes in (he he he). Seriously, English language publications are the best place to start, or perhaps you fancy a radio broadcast. Whatever you choose make sure the magazine or radio station you decide upon is locally based as I imagine this is where most of your customers will be situated. There's no harm also in scouting some of the other businesses in your area that you know your target audience frequent. Chat to the owner and ask if you can leave some leaflets or a business card in their premises. Many English bars, for example, have a notice board for the purpose of attaching information on businesses catering for ex-pats in the area.

6. Inject time.

You must be prepared to churn in a lot of initial time and effort to make your business a success. It's not going to grow if you are sunbathing on the beach every day. You must allow at least one year or 18 months of hard graft to really see the results you want. When it is running nicely, then is the time to consider taking on an employee or two!

7. Don't be disheartened.

Not all businesses produce results straight away. Some take more work than others. But the most important thing is to stay strong and continue believing, even on the bad days. If you don't think you can do this, then forget it right now.

8. Use positive thought tactics.

This is the point where many of you will think I'm raving loony mad, but positive thought techniques really will help your business to succeed. It is all to do with the Law of Attraction, which I wrote about at points throughout this book. To really understand how it works you are better off buying another book on the subject. Essentially it means you can get whatever you want through mere thought. Sounds bizarre I know, but it really works.

Trust me, I'm a magazine Editor…!

Perhaps I'll write a future book addressing the subject of the Law of Attraction in greater depth.

Good luck to all those who embark on a new business. And if you fancy running your very own *The Sentinella* magazine, then see the next page!

The Sentinella Global Magazine Network

Would you like to run your very own *The Sentinella* magazine in an area and country to suit?

Whether you fancy a move to Spain, Portugal, France, or even Dubai, this easy to run business would be ideal! Even if you prefer to stay in the UK, the opportunities  there are also endless, and there's no need for you to have had any experience in running a magazine before, as we show you exactly how to do it.

We provide all the help and support you will need, including training days, a fully comprehensive and easy to follow training guide, computer programmes and text books, and even a template of *The Sentinella* magazine. All the hard work has already been done for you! You also receive branded stationery, a USB stick containing all the documents you will possibly need and back issues of *The Sentinella* for simplifying your advertising sales.

All you need to do is pay a one off fee for the opportunity and a small license fee every month.

About The Author

Keidi Keating, now twenty-eight, began writing at the age of seven when she penned a series of children's tales.

After moving to Spain in 2004, Keidi began writing a diary to record her feelings and experiences. Reviewing it a few years later, she realised what a journey she had endured and decided to share this with others considering a move abroad. After a lot of hard work, *Sol Searching* was born!

Keidi is Editor of *The Sentinella* magazine, a popular A5 sized publication distributed in the Axarquia region of Spain, east of Málaga. She is also Director of *The Sentinella Global Magazine Network*, which offers people the chance to launch *The Sentinella* in their preferred location.

For more information about *The Sentinella* magazine log on to *www.thesentinella.com*

Also available from
www.nativespain.com

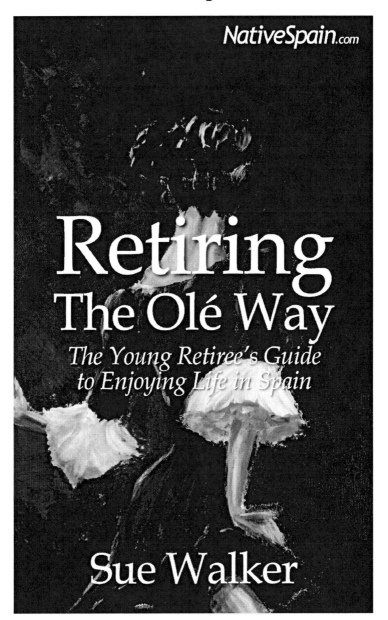

NativeSpain.com

Retiring
The Olé Way
*The Young Retiree's Guide
to Enjoying Life in Spain*

Sue Walker

Also available from
www.nativespain.com

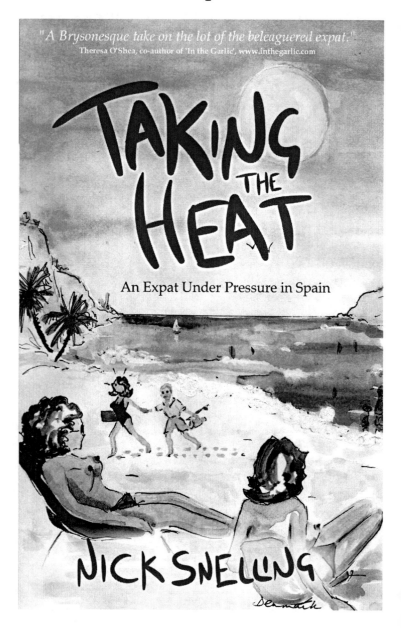

"*A Brysonesque take on the lot of the beleaguered expat.*"
Theresa O'Shea, co-author of 'In the Garlic', www.inthegarlic.com

TAKING
THE
HEAT

An Expat Under Pressure in Spain

NICK SNELLING

Also available from
www.nativespain.com

NativeSpain.com

Deborah Fletcher

CPSIA information can be obtained at www.ICGtesting.com
Printed in the USA
LVOW102117090912

298085LV00008B/25/P